D1329818

OBSERVATIONS ON THE GROWTH OF THE MIND

OBSERVATIONS

ON THE

GROWTH OF THE MIND

WITH REMARKS ON

SOME OTHER SUBJECTS

(1838)

BY

SAMPSON REED

A FACSIMILE REPRODUCTION
WITH AN INTRODUCTION
BY

CARL F. STRAUCH

GAINESVILLE, FLORIDA
SCHOLARS' FACSIMILES & REPRINTS
1970

SCHOLARS' FACSIMILES & REPRINTS
1605 N.W. 14TH AVENUE
GAINESVILLE, FLORIDA, 32601, U.S.A.
HARRY R. WARFEL, GENERAL EDITOR

REPRODUCED FROM A COPY IN

AND WITH THE PERMISSION OF

HARVARD UNIVERSITY LIBRARY

L. C. CATALOG CARD NUMBER: 78-100126
SBN 8201-1070-1

MANUFACTURED IN THE U.S.A.

INTRODUCTION

In 1886 the Reverend James Reed brought out the eighth American edition of his father's *Observations on the Growth of the Mind.* In a short biographical preface he sketched Sampson Reed's career as a Harvard undergraduate, theological student, and druggist. "The 'Growth of the Mind'," said James Reed, "was first published in 1826, when its author was but twenty-six years of age. It was written at odd moments during the intervals of business as an apothecary. He first offered it to the 'North American Review'; but the editor, Jared Sparks, declined it . . . and advised publication as a separate volume."

The little book was published on August 29 by

Cummings, Hilliard and Company, and it is most unlikely that in the succeeding months and years there was a more perceptive and enthusiastic reader than Ralph Waldo Emerson. On September 10 he wrote in his journal, "Our American press does not often issue such productions as Sampson Reed's observations on the Growth of the mind, a book . . . remarkable for the unity into which it has resolved the various powers, feelings & vocations of men, suggesting to the mind that harmony which it has always a propensity to seek of action & design in the order of providence in the world." " 'Tis droll," he wrote his brother William, September 29, "but it was all writ in the shop." The results, nonetheless, were sublime, for *Growth of the Mind* was "a noble pamphlet after my own heart . . . in my poor judgment the best thing since Plato of Plato's kind, for novelty & wealth of truth." Emerson's letter of September 23 to his maiden aunt Mary Moody Emerson must have reflected his reading in *Growth of the Mind,* a copy of which he sent her, for in her letter to him, September 25, she commented sharply that she found triteness, obscurity, and "swedenishness" in it, and she thought its best parts taken from Wordsworth. She was possibly led to this conclusion by the quotation on the title page from Wordsworth's *The Excursion*:

So build we up the Being that we are;
Thus deeply drinking-in the Soul of Things
We shall be wise perforce; and while inspired
By choice, and conscious that the will is free,
Unswerving shall we move, as if impell'd
By strict necessity, along the path
Of order and of good.

Others were more sympathetic than the dour Aunt Mary. In 1833 on his visit to Carlyle at Craigenputtock Emerson mentioned Reed and in the following year sent Carlyle a copy of "the little book of my Swedenborgian druggist, of whom I told you." In his first letter to Emerson, Carlyle responded favorably. "He is a faithful thinker that Swedenborgian Druggist of yours, with really deep Ideas, who makes me to pause and think, were it only to consider what manner of man *he* must be, and what manner of thing, after all, Swedenborgianism must be." In "Count Cagliostro," printed in *Fraser's Magazine*, August, 1833, Carlyle had considered Swedenborgians mere quacks, and his remarks to Emerson, therefore, show an altered view. But Carlyle went further, and in a letter to J. J. G. Wilkinson, the English Swedenborgian, he made handsome amends: "But I have been rebuked already; a little book, by one Sampson Reed, of Boston, in New England, which some friend sent hither, taught me that a Swedenborgian may have thoughts of the calmest kind on the deepest things; that in short, I did *not* know Swedenborg, and ought to know him." The first London edition of *Growth of the Mind* had appeared in 1827, and Carlyle's praise inspired a second London edition in 1839.

Emerson's proselytizing fervor extended to James Freeman Clarke, who in 1833 had gone west to Louisville to be pastor of a newly established Unitarian congregation and who subsequently was to become a leading Transcendentalist. "Have you read Sampson Reed's 'Growth of the Mind'?" asked Emerson in a letter of 1834. "I rejoice to be contemporary with that man, and cannot wholly despair of the society in which he lives. . . ." In 1844 Emerson made a gift of the second Boston edition of 1829 to a Scottish acquaintance, Dr. Samuel Brown; and many years later, in 1882, Alexander H. Japp, in his essay, "A Gift from Emerson," contributed to the *Gentleman's Magazine*, said that this copy had come into his possession, and, far more important, he proceeded to demonstrate that "this little unambitious book, by one whose name is now hardly remembered, had *some* share in the building up of the genius of Emerson." Reed had influenced Emerson in the cardinal doctrines that nature is the symbol of spirit and that the universe is the externization of the soul. Reed had made much of the Swedenborgian doctrine that each person has his "peculium," his "use," in the exercise of which he may best develop his character, and Emerson followed him in this. Reed viewed the power and function of poetry morally, and Emerson made a similar stress. So went Japp's argument; but it is easy to see today, almost a hundred years later, that, however correct Japp was, he could not affect the reputation that was being developed for Emerson from James Eliot Cabot to Oscar Firkins, a period of almost forty years of largely biographical account and superficial interpretation that omitted all but the greatest influences.

Beginning with the 1920's intensive scholarship has brought Reed to light once again, and in the work of Sutcliffe, Hotson, and Cameron the great indebtedness of Emerson to Reed has been disclosed—one may hope, permanently.

But *Growth of the Mind* and its author have an importance beyond that of contributing ideas and a vocabulary to Emerson; the book is an important document in the history of American Transcendentalism. The third American edition, which was published on Tuesday, May 1, 1838, and which is here reproduced in facsimile, contained a preface that momentarily lessened Emerson's respect for Reed though not for his ideas.

The rift between the two men was doubtless prepared by Reed's review in the *New Jerusalem Magazine* for October, 1837, of Emerson's "The American Scholar." Emerson regarded Swedenborg as a literary man, not a religious leader, and thought that his attempt to "engraft a purely philosophical Ethics on the popular Christianity of his time" a failure. For Emerson the immense value of Swedenborg lay in his "piercing the emblematic or spiritual character of the visible, audible, tangible world." Reed took exception to this attitude and these remarks; and though he conceded that Emerson "intended to speak respectfully and truly of Swedenborg . . . his remarks show that he has read him little; —or rather, to little purpose." Here I need not anticipate Reed's indictment of Transcendentalism in his preface except to observe that such a sentence as the following does forcefully exhibit the author's view that we should speak the truth rather than attempt to please: "*Transcendentalism* is the parasite of *sensualism;* and when it shall have done its work, it will be found to be itself a worm, and the offspring of a worm." Reed's unflattering remarks contributed to Emerson's impatience with sectarian narrowness and thus provide us with important background for the "Divinity School Address." In a significant journal passage in June on Sampson Reed, Emerson commented on "the malign influences of this immense arrogancy & subtle bigotry of his church." At about the same time Emerson must have written his poem "S. R.", which he never published but which I have recently printed with commentary. In it Emerson deplored Reed's falling away from the ideal vision of youth, his declining "the strife of virtue" and becoming one of the "placid rich men," a "Sleek deacon of the New Jerusalem."

What of the book itself? Reed's purpose in *Growth of the Mind* was to establish a basis for church doctrine in the metaphysical structure of the universe as that is disclosed in law—laws of nature, mind, science, and poetry, laws that are "fixed and perfect." Thus, whatever the Swedenborgian impress and intent, *Growth of the Mind* is a minor classic of Romantic naturalism, exhibiting the same effort found in more famous works of the period to make a synthesis of metaphysics, epistemology, science, and poetry. Reed's metaphysics becomes a psychology when he introduces the organic metaphor in his remark that "the mind must grow, not from external accretion, but from an internal principle" and further that "the infant mind should possess the germ of every science." "Do we love to gaze on the sun, the moon, the stars, and the planets? This affection contains in its bosom the whole science of astronomy." The universe is a dynamic organism, and science must therefore be taught as a living thing. Like science and man himself, poetry is rooted in nature, and Reed accordingly repudiates poetic art; when he says that poetry is not versification or fiction and dismisses rime as unnatural and as possessing "too strongly the marks of art," Reed anticipates Whitman as radically as Emerson.

Of interest is Reed's stress on the individuality, the unique quality of every species of creation. "There is a language, not of words but of things. . . . But everything which is, whether animal or vegetable, is full of the expression of that use for which it is designed, as of its own existence. . . . Let a man's language be confined to the expression of that which actually belongs to his own mind; and let him respect the smallest blade which grows and permit it to speak for itself." No other religious writer, certainly no other Romantic, was more profoundly aware of a universe of individual existences, each justified in its "peculium" or "use." "It becomes us then to seek and to cherish," observed Reed in bringing his pamphlet to a close, "this *peculium* of our own minds, as the patrimony which is left us by our Father in heaven . . . as the forming power within us, which gives to our persons that by which they are distinguished from others. . . ."

Much of the early Emerson is here in germ, the concern for the nature of language, the assertion of a divine self-reliance, the incipient symbolism. Emerson's indebtedness to Reed has for some time been a matter of record even though in his far-ranging quest for confirmation of his own moods and convictions Emerson went beyond Reed.

It is much too easy to discuss Reed only in relation to Emerson, and apart from the injustice to Reed, this narrow perspective excludes the rebellious generation to which both belonged. Transcendentalism was a loose confederation of young men and women so individualistic that they may be said to have agreed fully on only one matter—their opposition to the entrenched Lockean and Unitarian order. Though no Transcendentalist, Reed belonged to the rebellion and in the unfolding of American thought can be understood best as a young and ardent seeker, one among many, for a more poetical and humane view of man and the world than the established order provided.

Born in Bridgewater, Massachusetts, on June 10, 1800, Sampson Reed was the son of the Reverend John Reed, a Unitarian clergyman, who had served in Congress during the Presidency of Washington. Educated in his earlier years by his father, he entered Harvard in 1814, where he met Thomas Worcester, five years his senior. Worcester was reading Swedenborg and imparted his knowledge to his fellow students. Reed and Worcester graduated in 1818 and entered the Divinity School, where together with John H. Wilkins they continued in their New-Church tendencies. In 1820 Reed and Wilkins were formally admitted into the Boston New-Church Society, of which Worcester, already a member, became pastor in 1821. On August 21, 1821, Reed delivered his "Oration on Genius," so inspring to Emerson, for the M.A. at the Harvard Commencement, when Emerson himself graduated. Much later, in 1849, it was to be printed in *Aesthetic Papers,* edited by Elizabeth P. Peabody. For a period of three years Reed was apprenticed to the druggist William B. White, and sometime during 1825 Reed opened his own retail drug store, which subsequently, in partnership with Dr. Abram T. Lowe, he converted into a wholesale firm. In January, 1861, he retired and gave his interest in the business to his son Thomas. His career was eminently successful in business, public service, and church activities. When he died in 1880 an obituary commented on the early conversion of a number of young men to the Swedenborgian faith, of whom Reed was one. "With hardly an exception, these young men became prosperous and even wealthy."

During his apprenticeship Reed had been concerned about the gap between the apothecary shop and what he thought his true spiritual vocation should be. In a letter to Theophilus Parsons, March 6, 1823, he wrote, "It is but lately that I have thought I could discover in my own mind, any thing like an essential, incipient use, by which the two things will be united." "Reed did eventually find his use," says Cameron, "chiefly as a writer and apologist for the Swedenborgian way of life." Reed helped to found the *New Jerusalem Magazine*, the first number of which appeared in September, 1827. Throughout his life he was a frequent contributor, and for the third edition of *Growth of the Mind* he gathered a handful of essays that best represented his work during the first decade of the periodical.

These eight selections are of varying interest, but as theological writings embracing an entire system of God, the world, man, and animals, they possess an antique charm and poetic truth that appealed powerfully to Emerson's imagination. The ground-plan of all Reed's work is the correspondence between the physical and the spiritual, and so it is of all Emerson's. If Reed did not write literature he prepared the materials for it as Emerson absorbed him together with a host of other such inspirers. It indicates a vigor in *Growth of the Mind* that from 1826 to 1886 it went through ten editions, eight in the United States and two in England. Altogether the third edition is a landmark in American thought and provides the student with a convenient starting point for the exploration of Reed's prolific output.

For the convenience of the student I append a bibliographical listing of Reed's selections from the *New Jerusalem Magazine* in the order in which they occur in the third edition of *Observations on the Growth of the Mind;* where titles vary I give the title as it occurs in *NJM*:

"Miracles," I (January, 1828), 148-156.
"Conscience," V (January, 1832), 186-191.
"Home," V (May, 1832), 350-352.
"Self-Love Essential Evil," IV (May, 1831), 338-346.
"External Restraint," VI (September, 1832), 30-32.
"Hereditary Evil," VII (November, 1833), 97-99.
"Marriage in the Heavens," V (May, 1832), 321-328.
"Lessons for Children of the New Church," X (May, 1837), 298-310.

CARL F. STRAUCH

Lehigh University
July 9, 1969

OBSERVATIONS

ON THE

GROWTH OF THE MIND;

WITH REMARKS ON

SOME OTHER SUBJECTS.

BY SAMPSON REED.

BOSTON:
PUBLISHED BY OTIS CLAPP,
121 Washington Street.
1838.

PRINTED BY MANNING AND FISHER,

No. 8 Congress Street.

CONTENTS.

PREFACE.

"The Growth of the Mind" has now been through two editions in this country, and one in England. It has been received with a degree of favor, though not great, yet sufficient to make me sometimes distrustful of its merit; and frequently apprehensive that its meaning was not fully understood and received. That this has sometimes been the case, I have known to be the fact.

So far as an author duly feels in whose presence he stands, it can be no source of gratification to him to attract personal admiration or praise. He must regard himself as only a medium of truth from the one only Source of truth, and the forms in which he has been permitted to present it, as useful only so far as they are suitable vessels to contain and to communicate it. Truth itself—simple—unadorned—divine—is at the present day revealed, yet noticed and loved by few. The King of Kings and Lord of Lords is standing in the midst of us; "but he hath no form nor comeliness; and when we shall see him, there is no beauty that we should desire him." The spiritual sense of the Sacred Scripture is opened; "yet is it despised and rejected of men."

The present age is characterized by the love of

pleasing, as opposed to the love of truth. Fashionable education, as it is often pursued, may almost be defined the cultivation of the art of pleasing. This is but too frequently the end for which so much labor is bestowed, by which a wardrobe of accomplishments is provided, which may be used as occasion requires. When the disposition to please takes the first place, it is obvious that truth must be sought only as it is subservient to this object. "How can ye believe who seek honor one of another, and seek not that honor which cometh from God only." The love of pleasing is opposed to the love of truth, when a person desires to please others, in order that he may gain an influence over them, for the sake of promoting his own private ends or personal advantage. The love of pleasing is consistent with the love of truth, when a person desires to please, for the sake of promoting the good of others, and the cause of truth itself.

The New Church can discern, in almost every moral or religious writer of any acknowledged merit at the present day, some outbreakings of its own power; while its principles are pressing into the natural sciences, like so many gushing fountains from an inexhaustible fountain above them. It is painful to see how little willingness there is to acknowledge the source of truth; and how often a man seems to think that it has answered its legitimate purpose, when he has bedecked his own person therewith, so as to command the admiration of the multitude.

But the time is approaching when the claims of the New Church on the public attention may not be easily set aside. There is a problem to solve, to which those who reject the claims of this Church, will find it difficult to furnish a solution; and the misrepresentations and ignorance which have often prevailed in regard to it, will, before many years, be seen to be neither consistent with good manners nor good scholarship. The writings of Swedenborg are so pure in their character and influence, that the moral sense of the community will bear testimony that there is no wilful imposture; and they are so perfect in their method and logic, that the rationality of the community will bear testimony that there is no insanity. The voice of these two witnesses cannot be silenced; and the day is approaching, when the assertion that these writings are not of sufficient importance to command the attention of the public, will not be hazarded by any one, who either is a man of intelligence or seeks to be so esteemed.

Still the natural mind is ever backward to receive *revealed truth*, both from the character of this truth itself, and from the fact of its being revealed—from the character of the truth, because it is opposed to the affections and principles of the natural mind, and calculated to reform and regenerate them—from the fact of its being revealed, because it leaves no place for the pride of discovery. "Whosoever will, let him take the water of life freely." The water of life is really as free as natural water; and this we all know is the common gift of Providence to man and beast. But the condition is, that we should *will to receive it*—that we should acknowledge it to be the water of life, and endeavor to live from it—that we should seek to be purified and regenerated by its influence. And alas! how few are disposed to comply with these conditions, and how much do these find in themselves, which requires to be subdued and put away!

From these causes it is not to be expected that the truths of the spiritual sense of the Sacred Scripture, which the Lord has now revealed through his servant Emanuel Swedenborg, will find a very ready reception. *Transcendentalism** will rather be caressed. This is the product of man's own brain; and when the human mind has been compelled to relax its grasp on sensualism, and the philosophy based on the senses, it may be expected first to take refuge here. *Transcendentalism*, even now, offers indications of an approaching popularity in this country. It may be something gained, when the idolater no longer literally worships the work of his own hands; even though he be in heart an idola-

* By *transcendentalism*, I mean such transcendentalism as we now find, without any reference to its origin, or to the original meaning of the word.

ter still, and worship the creations of his own imagination. So it may be a step forwards from *sensualism* to *transcendentalism*. It may be a necessary step in the progress of the human mind. But they still lie near each other—almost in contact. There is among insects a class called parasites. Their instinct leads them to deposit their eggs in the bodies of other insects, where, when the young is hatched, it has only to open its mouth and eat up its brother. It would seem to be in a way analogous to this, that Providence often permits one falsity to be removed by another. *Transcendentalism* is the parasite of *sensualism;* and when it shall have done its work, it will be found to be itself a worm, and the offspring of a worm.

The Sacred Scripture is the only door through which we can enter into life, or receive living truths; and all who would climb up any other way are thieves and robbers. Imagining themselves spiritual, it is possible that they should be even the lowest of the sensual—for they may only give to their sensuality wings, by which it may gain an apparent elevation without any real change in its nature—superadding to its inherent properties that of monstrosity—becoming a winged serpent—the monstrous offspring of the infernal influence and a vain imagination. "On thy belly shalt thou go, and dust shalt thou eat, all the days of thy life," is with the serpent the law of its nature; and any attempt to *transcend* this law must rather debase than elevate it. If it presume to raise itself into the air, and live on the nectar of flowers, its real quality will become the more apparent and disgusting—it will only defile what can afford it no nutriment, and all the birds of heaven will instinctively shun its company. Let every one know, therefore, that his real faith in the Sacred Scripture and humble dependence upon it for life and light, are the only measure of his spirituality—that whatever seems to abound more than these, is nothing, or worse than nothing. Such "sons of the morning" may be expected in these latter times—for the morning has indeed come, and, with the beginning of a brighter day than the world has yet seen, are awakened into life forms as monstrous as those of the dark ages.

In conclusion, I would dedicate this volume to the New Church and to those who are approaching it. By the approbation of that Church I shall always be strengthened, and encouraged by the approbation of those who are not of the Church, so far as it affords indications that they are drawing near to it. I have been cheered by a knowlege of the fact, that in some instances, at least, this book has been instrumental in directing the feet of the reader to the "New Jerusalem, which is descending from God out of heaven." S. R.

BOSTON, FEB. 28, 1838.

OBSERVATIONS

ON THE

GROWTH OF THE MIND.

NOTHING is a more common subject of remark than the changed condition of the world. There is a more extensive intercourse of thought, and a more powerful action of mind upon mind, than formerly. The good and the wise of all nations are brought nearer together, and begin to exert a power, which, though yet feeble as infancy, is felt throughout the globe. Public opinion, that helm which directs the progress of events by which the world is guided to its ultimate destination, has received a new direction. The mind has attained an upward and onward look, and is shaking off the errors and prejudices of the past. The structure of the feudal ages, the ornament of the desert, has been exposed to the light of heaven; and continues to be gazed at for its ugliness, as it ceases to be admired for its antiquity. The world is deriving vigor, not from that which is gone by, but from that which is coming; not from the unhealthy moisture of the evening, but from the nameless influences of the morning. The loud call on the past to instruct us, as it falls on the rock of ages, comes back in echo from the future. Both mankind, and the laws and principles by which they are governed, seem about to be redeemed from slavery. The moral and intellectual character of man has undergone, and is undergoing, a change; and as this is effected, it must change the aspect of all things, as when the position-point is altered from which a landscape is viewed. We appear to be approaching an age which will be the silent pause of merely physical force before the powers of the mind; the timid, subdued, awed condition of the brute, gazing on the erect and godlike form of man.

These remarks with respect to the present era are believed to be just, when it is viewed on the bright side. They are not made by one who is insensible to its evils. Least of all, are they intended to countenance that feeling of self-admiration, which carries with it the seeds of premature disease and deformity; for to be proud of the truth is to cease to possess it. Since the fall of man, nothing has been more difficult for him than to know his real condition, since every departure from divine order is attended with a loss of the knowledge of what it is. When our first parents left the garden of Eden, they took with them no means by which they might measure the depths of degradation to which they fell; no chart by which they might determine their moral longitude. Most of our knowledge implies relation and comparison. It is not difficult for one age, or one individual, to be compared with another; but this determines only their relative condition. The actual condition of man can be seen only from the relation in which he stands to his immutable Creator; and this relation is discovered from the light of revelation, so far as, by conforming to the precepts of revelation, it is permitted to exist according to the laws of divine order. It is not sufficient that the letter of the Bible is in the world. This may be, and still mankind continue in ignorance of themselves. It must be obeyed from the heart to the hand. The book must be eat, and constitute the living flesh. When only the relative condition of the world is regarded, we are apt to exult over other ages and other men, as if we ourselves were a different order of beings, till at length we are enveloped in the very mists from which we are proud of being cleared. But when the relative state of the world is justly viewed from the real state of the individual, the scene is lighted from the point of the beholder with the chaste light of humility which never deceives; it is not forgotten that the way lies forward; the cries of exultation cease to be heard in the march of progression, and the mind, in whatever it learns of the past and the present, finds food for improvement, and not for vain-glory.

As all the changes which are taking place in the world originate in the mind, it might be naturally expected that nothing would change more than the mind itself, and whatever is connected with a description of it. While men have been speculating concerning their own powers, the sure but secret influence of revelation has been gradually changing the moral and intellectual character of the world, and the ground on which they were standing has passed from under them, almost while their words were in their mouths. The powers of the mind are most intimately connected with the subjects by which they are occupied. We cannot think of the will without feeling, of the understanding without thought, or of the imagination without something like poetry. The mind is visible when it is active; and as the subjects on which it is engaged are changed, the powers themselves present a different aspect. New classifications arise, and new names are given. What was considered simple, is thought to consist of distinct parts, till at length the philosopher hardly knows whether the African be of the same or a different species; and though the soul is thought to continue after death, angels are universally considered a distinct class of intellectual beings. Thus it is that there is nothing fixed in the philosophy of the mind; it is said to be a science which is not demonstrative; and though now thought to be brought to a state of great perfection, another century, under the providence of God, and nothing will be found in the structure which has cost so much labor, but the voice "he is not here, but is risen."

Is then everything that relates to the immortal part of man fleeting and evanescent, while the laws of physical nature remain unaltered? Do things become changeable as we approach the immutable and the eternal? Far otherwise. The laws of the mind are in themselves as fixed and perfect as the laws of matter; but they are laws from which we have wandered. There is a philosophy of the mind, founded not on the aspect it presents in any part or in any period of the world, but on its immutable relations to its first cause; a philosophy equally applicable to man, before or after he has passed the valley of the shadow of death; not dependent on time or place, but immortal as its subject. The light of this philosophy has begun to beam faintly on the world, and mankind will yet see their own moral and intellectual nature by the light of revelation, as it shines through the moral and intellectual character it shall have itself created. It may be remarked, also, that the changes in the sciences and the arts are entirely the effect of revelation. To revelation it is to be ascribed, that the genius which has taught the laws of the heavenly bodies and analyzed the material world, did not spend itself in drawing the bow or in throwing the lance, in the chase or in war; and that the vast powers of Handel did not burst forth in the wild notes of the war-song. It is the tendency of revelation to give a right direction to every power of every mind; and when this is effected, inventions and discoveries will follow of course, all things assume a different aspect, and the world itself again become a paradise.

It is the object of the following pages not to be influenced by views of a temporal or local nature, but to look at the mind as far as possible in its essential revealed character, and, beginning with its powers of acquiring and retaining truth, to trace summarily that development which is required, in order to render it truly useful and happy.

It is said, *the powers of acquiring and retaining truth*, because truth is not retained without some continued exertion of the same powers by which it is acquired. There is the most intimate connection of the memory with the affections. This connection is obvious from many familiar expressions; such as remember me to any one, by which is signified a desire to be borne in his or her affections—do not forget me, by which is meant do not cease to love me—get by heart, which means commit to memory. It is also obvious from observation of our own minds; from the constant recurrence of those subjects which we most love, and the extreme difficulty of detaching our own minds or the minds of others from a favorite pursuit. It is obvious from the power of attention on which the memory principally depends, which, if the subject have a place in our affections, requires no effort; if it have not, the effort consists principally in giving it a real or an artificial hold of our feelings, as it is possible, if we do not love a subject, to attend to it, because it may add to our fame or our wealth. It is obvious from the never-fading freshness retained by the scenes of childhood, when the feelings are strong and vivid, through the later periods of life. As the old man looks back on the road of his pilgrimage, many years of active life lie unseen in the valley, as his eye rests on the rising ground of his younger days; presenting a beautiful illustration of the manner in which the human mind, when revelation shall have accomplished its work, shall no longer regard the scene of sin and misery behind, but having completed the circle, shall rest, as next to the present moment, on the golden age, the infancy of the world. The connection of the memory with the affections is also obvious from the association of ideas; since the train of thoughts suggested by any scene or event in any individual, depends on his own peculiar and prevailing feelings; as whatever enters into the animal system, wherever it may arise, seems first to be recognised as a part of the man, when it has found its way to the heart, and received from that its impulse. It is but a few years, (how strange to tell!) since man discovered that the blood circulated through the human body. We have, perhaps, hardly learned the true nature of that intellectual circulation, which gives life and health to the human mind. The affections are to the soul, what the heart is to the body. They send forth their treasures with a vigor not less powerful, though not material, throughout the intellectual man, strengthening and nourishing; and again receive those treasures to themselves, enlarged by the effect of their own operation.

Memory is the *effect* of learning, through whatever avenue it may have entered the mind. It is said, the *effect;* because the man who has read a volume, and can perhaps tell you nothing of its contents, but simply express his own views on the same subject with more clearness and precision, may as truly be said to have remembered, as he that can repeat the very words. In the one case, the powers of the mind have received a new tone; in the other, they are encumbered with a useless burthen—in the one, they are made stronger; in the other, they are more oppressed with weight—in the one, the food is absorbed and becomes a part of the man; in the other, it lies on the stomach in a state of crude indigestion.

There is no power more various in different individuals, than the memory. This may be ascribed to two reasons. First, this partakes of every power of the mind, since every mental exertion is a subject of memory, and may therefore be said to indicate all the difference that actually exists. Secondly, this power varies in its character as it has more or less to do with time. Simple divine truth has nothing to do with time. It is the same yesterday, to-day, and to-morrow. The memory of this is simply the development of the mind. But we are so surrounded by facts of a local and temporal nature; the place where, and the time when, make so great a part of what is presented to our consideration, that the attribute is mistaken for the subject; and this power sometimes appears to have exclusive reference to time, though, strictly speaking, it has no relation to it. There is a power of growth in the spiritual man, and if in his progress we be able to mark, as in the grain of the oak, the number of the years, this is only a circumstance, and all that is gained would be as real if no such lines existed. The mind ought not to be limited by the short period of its own duration in the body, with a beginning and end comprising a few years; it should be poised on its own immortality, and what is learned, should be learned with a view to that real adaptation of knowledge to the mind which results from the harmony of creation; and whenever or wherever we exist, it will be useful to us. The memory has, in reality, nothing to do with time, any more than the eye has with space. As the latter learns by experience to measure the distance of objects, so the consciousness of the present existence of states of mind, is referred to particular periods of the past. But when the soul has entered on its *eternal* state, there is reason to believe that the past and the future will be swallowed up in the present; that memory and anticipation will be lost in consciousness; that everything of the past will be comprehended in the present. without any reference to time, and everything of the future will exist in the divine effort of progression.

What is time? There is perhaps no question that would suggest such a variety of answers. It is represented to us from our infancy as producing such important changes, both in destroying some, and in healing the wounds it has inflicted on others, that people generally imagine, if not an actual person, it is at least a real existence. We begin with time in the Primer, and end with reasoning about the foreknowledge of God. What is time? The difficulty of answering the question, (and there are few questions more difficult,) arises principally from our having ascribed so many important effects to that which has no real existence. It is true that all things in the natural world are subject to change. But however these changes may be connected in our minds with time, it requires but a moment's reflection to see that time has no agency in them. They are the effects of chemical, or more properly, perhaps, of natural decompositions and reorganizations. Time, or rather our idea of it, so far from having produced anything, is itself the effect of changes. There are certain operations in nature, which, depending on fixed laws, are in themselves perfectly regular; if all things were equally so, the question how long? might never be asked. We should never speak of a late season, or of premature old age; but everything passing on in an invariable order, all the idea of time that would remain with respect to any object, would be a sort of instinctive sense of its condition, its progress or decay. But most of the phenomena in the natural world are exceedingly irregular; for though the same combination of causes would invariably produce the same effect, the same combination very rarely occurs. Hence, in almost every change, and we are conversant with nothing but changes, we are assisted in ascertaining its nature and extent, by referring it to something in itself perfectly regular. We find this regularity in the apparent motions of the sun and moon. It is difficult to tell how much our idea of time is the effect of artificial means of keeping it, and what would be our feelings on the subject, if left to the simple operations of nature

—but they would probably be little else than a reference of all natural phenomena to that on which they principally depend, the relative situation of the sun and earth; and the idea of an actual succession of moments would be, in a measure, resolved into that of cause and effect.

Eternity is to the mind what time is to nature. We attain a perception of it, by regarding all the operations in the world within us, as they exist in relation to their first cause; for in doing this, they are seen to partake somewhat of the nature of that Being on whom they depend. We make no approaches to a conception of it, by heaping day upon day or year upon year. This is merely an accumulation of time; and we might as well attempt to convey an idea of mental greatness by that of actual space, as to communicate a conception of eternity by years or thousands of years. Mind and matter are not more distinct from each other then their properties; and by an attempt to embrace all time, we are actually farther from an approach to eternity than when we confine ourselves to a single instant; because we merely collect the largest possible amount of natural changes, whereas that which is eternal approaches that which is immutable. This resembles the attempt to ascend to heaven by means of the tower of Babel, in which they were removed by their pride from that which they would have approached, precisely in proportion to their apparent progress. It is impossible to conceive of either time or space without matter. The reason is, they are the effect of matter; and as it is by creating matter that they are produced, so it is by thinking of it that they are conceived of. It need not be said how exceedingly improper it is to apply the usual ideas of time and space to the Divine Being; making him subject to that which he creates.

Still our conceptions of time, of hours, days or years, are among the most vivid we possess, and we neither wish nor find it easy to call them in question. We are satisfied with the fact, that time is indicated on the face of the watch, without seeking for it among the wheels and machinery. But what is the idea of a year? Every natural change that comes under our observation leaves a corresponding impression on the mind; and the sum of the changes which come under a single revolution of the earth round the sun, conveys the impression of a year. Accordingly, we find that our idea of a year is continually changing, as the mind becomes conversant with different objects, and is susceptible of different impressions; and the days of the old man, as they draw near their close, seem to gather rapidity from their approach to the other world. We have all experienced the effect of pleasure and pain in accelerating and retarding the passing moments; and since our feelings are constantly changing, we have no reason to doubt that they constantly produce a similar effect, though it may not be often noticed. The divisions of time, then, however real they may seem to be, and however well they may serve the common purposes of conversation, cannot be supposed to convey the same impression to any two minds, nor to any one mind in different periods of its existence. Indeed, unless this were the fact, all artificial modes of keeping it would be unnecessary. Time, then, is nothing real so far as it exists in our own minds.

Nor do we find a nearer approach to reality by any analysis of nature. Everything, as was said, is subject to change, and one change prepares the way for another; by which there is growth and decay. There are also motions of bodies, both in nature and art, which in their operation observe fixed laws; and here we end. The more we enter into an analysis of things, the farther are we from finding anything that answers to the distinctness and reality which are usually attached to a conception of time, and there is reason to believe that when this distinctness and reality are most deeply rooted, (whatever may be the theory,) they are uniformly attended with a practical belief of the actual motion of the sun, and are indeed the effect of it. Let us then continue to talk of time, as we talk of the rising and setting of the sun; but let us think rather of those changes in their origin and effect, from which a sense of time is produced. This will carry us one degree nearer the actual condition of things; it will admit us one step further into the temple of creation—no longer a temple created six thousand years ago, and deserted by him who formed it; but a temple with the hand of the builder resting upon it, perpetually renewing, perpetually creating—and as we bow ourselves to worship the "I AM," "Him who liveth forever and ever, who created heaven and the things that are therein, and the earth and the things that are therein, and the sea and the things that are therein," we may hear in accents of divine love the voice that proclaims "that there shall be time no longer."

It is not the living productions of nature, by which the strongest impression of time is produced. The oak, over which may have passed a hundred years, seems to drive from our minds the impression of time, by the same power by which it supports its own life, and resists every tendency to decay. It is that which is decayed, though it may have been the offspring of an hour; it is the ruined castle mouldering into dust, still more, if the contrast be strengthened by its being covered with the living productions of nature; it is the half consumed remains of some animal once strong and vigorous, the discoveries of the undertaker, or the filthy relics of the catacomb, by which the strongest impression of time is conveyed. So it is with the possessions of the mind. It is that which is not used, which seems farthest in the memory, and which is held by the most doubtful tenure; that which is suffered to waste and decay because it wants the life of our own affections; that which we are about to lose, because it does not properly belong to us: whereas that truth, which is applied to the use and service of mankind, acquires a higher polish the more it is thus employed, like the angels of heaven, who forever approximate to a state of perfect youth, beauty, and innocence It is not a useless task, then, to remove from our minds the usual ideas of time, and cultivate a memory of things. It is to leave the mind in the healthy, vigorous and active possession of all its attainments, and exercise of all its powers; it is to remove from it, that only which contains the seeds of decay and putrefaction; to separate the living from the dead; to take from it the veil by which it would avoid the direct presence of Jehovah, and preserve its own possessions without using them.

Truth, all truth, is practical. It is impossible, from its nature and origin, that it should be otherwise. Whether its effect be directly to change the conduct, or it simply leave an impression on the heart, it is in the strictest sense practical. It should rather be our desire to use what we learn, than to remember it. If we desire to use it, we shall remember it of course; if we wish merely to remember, it is possible we may never use it. It is the tendency of all truth to effect some object. If we look at this object, it will form a distinct and permanent image on the mind; if we look merely at the truth, it will vanish away, like rays of light falling into vacancy.

Keeping in view what has been said on the subject of time, then, the mind is presented to us, as not merely active in the acquirement of truth, but active in its possession. The memory is the fire of the vestal virgins, sending forth perpetual light; not the grave which preserves simply because annihilation is impossible. The reservoir of knowledge should be seated in the affections, sending forth its influence throughout the mind, and terminating in word and deed, if I may be allowed the expression, merely because its channels and outlets are situated below the water-mark. There prevails a most erroneous sentiment, that the mind is originally vacant, and requires only to be filled up; and there is reason to believe, that this opinion is most intimately connected with false conceptions of time. The mind is originally a most delicate germ, whose husk is the body; planted in this world, that the light and heat of heaven may fall upon it with a gentle radiance, and call forth its energies. The process of learning is not by synthesis, or analysis. It is the most perfect illustration of both. As subjects are presented to the operation of the mind, they are decomposed and reorganized in a manner peculiar to itself, and not easily explained.

Another object of the preceding remarks upon time, is that we may be impressed with the immediate presence and agency of God, without which a correct understanding of mind or matter can never be attained; that we may be able to read on every power of the mind, and on every particle of matter, the language of our Lord, "My Father worketh hitherto, and I work." We usually put the Divine Being to an immense distance, by supposing that the world was created many years ago, and subjected to certain laws, by which it has since been governed. We find ourselves capable of constructing machines, which move on without our assistance, and imagine that the world was constructed in the same way. We forget that the motions of our machines depend on the uniform operation of what we call the laws of nature; and that there can be nothing beyond, on which these depend, unless it be the agency of that Being from whom they exist. The pendulum of the clock continues to move from the uniform operation of gravitation. It is no explanation, to say that it is a law of our machinery that the pendulum should move. We simply place things in a situation to be acted upon by an all-pervading power; but what all-pervading power is there by which gravitation is itself produced, unless it be the power of God?

The tendency of bodies to the earth, is something with which from our childhood we have been so familiar; something which we have regarded so much as a cause, since, in a certain sense, it is the cause of all the motions with which we are acquainted; that it is not agreeable to our habits of thinking, to look at it as an effect. Even the motions of the heavenly bodies seem completely accounted for, by simply extending to these phenomena, the feelings with which we have been accustomed to regard the tendency of bodies to the earth; whereas, if the two things were communicated at the same period of life, they would appear equally wonderful. An event appears to be explained, when it is brought within the pale of those youthful feelings and associations, which in their simplicity do not ask the reason of things. There is formed in the mind of the child, from his most familiar observations, however imperfect they may be, as it were a little nucleus, which serves as the basis of his future progress. This usually comprises a large proportion of those natural appearances, which the philosopher in later periods of life finds it most difficult to explain. The child grows up in his Father's house, and collects and arranges the most familiar operations and events. Into this collection he afterwards receives whatever history or science may communicate, and still feels at home; a feeling with which wonder is never associated.

This is not altogether as it should be. It is natural for the mature mind to ask the cause of things. It is unsatisfied when it does not find one, and can hardly exclude the thought of that Being, from whom all things exist. When therefore we have gone beyond the circle of youthful knowledge, and found a phenomenon in nature, which in its insulated state fills us with the admiration of God; let us beware how we quench this feeling. Let us rather transfer something of this admiration to those phenomena of the same class, which have not hitherto directed our minds beyond the fact of their actual existence. As the mind extends the boundaries of its knowledge, let a holy reference to God descend into its youthful treasures. That light which in the distance seemed to be a miraculous blaze, as it falls on our own native hills may still seem divine, but will not surprise us; and a sense of the constant presence of God will be happily blended with the most perfect freedom.

Till the time of Newton, the motion of the heavenly bodies was indeed a miracle. It was an event which stood alone, and was probably regarded with peculiar reference to the Divine Being. The feeling of worship with which they had previously been regarded, had subsided into a feeling of wonder; till at length they were received into the family of our most familiar associations. There is one step further. It is to regard gravitation, wherever it may be found, as an effect of the constant agency of the Divine Being, and from a consciousness of his presence and co-operation in every step we take, literally, "to walk humbly with our God." It is agreeable to the laws of moral and intellectual progression, that all phenomena, whether of matter or mind, should become gradually classified; till at length all things, wherever they are found; all events, whether of history or experience, of mind or matter; shall at once conspire to form one stupendous miracle, and cease to be such. They will form a miracle, in that they are seen to depend constantly and equally on the power of the

Lord; and they will cease to be a miracle, in that the power which pervades them, is so constant, so uniform, and so mild in its operation, that it produces nothing of fear, nothing of surprise. From whatever point we contemplate the scene, we feel that we are still in our Father's house; go where we will, the paternal roof, the broad canopy of heaven, is extended over us.

It is agreeable to our nature, that the mind should be particularly determined to one object. The eye appears to be the point at which the united rays of the sun within and the sun without, converge to an expression of unity; and accordingly the understanding can be conscious of but one idea or image at a time. Still there is another and a different kind of consciousness which pervades the mind, which is co-extensive with everything it actually possesses. There is but one object in nature on which the *eye* looks directly, but the whole body is pervaded with nerves which convey perpetual information of the existence and condition of every part. So it is with the possessions of the mind; and when an object ceases to be the subject of this kind of consciousness, it ceases to be remembered. The memory therefore, as was said, is not a dormant, but an active power. It is rather the possession than the retention of truth. It is a consciousness of the will; a consciousness of character; a consciousness which is produced by the mind's preserving in effort, whatever it actually possesses. It is the power which the mind has of preserving truth, without actually making it the subject of thought; bearing a relation to thought, analogous to what this bears to the actual perception of the senses, or to language. Thus we remember a distant object without actually thinking of it, in the same way that we think of it, without actually seeing it.

The memory is not limited, because to the affections, viewed simply as such, number is not applicable. They become distinct and are classified, when connected with truths, or, from being developed, are applied to their proper objects. Love may be increased, but not multiplied. A man may feel intensely, and the quantity and quality of his feeling may affect the character of his thought, but still it preserves its unity. The most ardent love is not attended with more than one idea, but on the contrary has a tendency to confine the mind to a single object. Every one must have remarked, that a peculiar state of feeling belongs to every exercise of the understanding; unless somewhat of this feeling remained after the thought had passed away, there would be nothing whereby the latter could be recalled. The impression thus left, exists continually in the mind; though, as different objects engage the attention, it may become less vivid. These impressions go to comprise the character of an individual; especially when they have acquired a reality and fixedness, in consequence of the feelings in which they originated, having resulted in the actions to which they tend. They enter into every subject about which we are thinking, and the particular modification they receive from that subject gives them the appearance of individuality; while they leave on the subject itself, the image of that character which they constitute. When a man has become acquainted with any science, that state of the affections which properly belongs to this science, (whatever direction his mind may take afterwards,) still maintains a certain influence; and this influence is the creative power by which his knowledge on the subject is reproduced. Such impressions are to the mind, what logarithms are in numbers; preserving our knowledge in its fulness indeed, but before it has expanded into an infinite variety of thoughts. Brown remarks, "we will the existence of certain ideas, it is said, and they arise in consequence of our volition; though assuredly to will any idea is to know that we will, and therefore to be conscious of that very idea, which we surely need not desire to know, when we already know it so well as to will its actual existence." The author does not discriminate between looking at an object and thence desiring it, and simply that condition of feeling between which and certain thoughts there is an established relation, so that the former cannot exist to any considerable degree without producing the latter. Of this exertion of the will, every one must have been conscious in his efforts of recollection. Of this exertion of the will, the priest must be conscious, when, (if he be sincere,) by the simple prostration of his heart before his Maker, his mind is crowded with the thoughts and language of prayer. Of this exertion of the will, the poet must be conscious, when he makes bare his bosom for the reception of nature, and presents her breathing with his own life and soul. But it is needless to illustrate that of which every one must be sensible.

It follows, from these views of the subject, that the true way to store the memory is to develope the affections. The mind must grow, not from external accretion, but from an internal principle. Much may be done by others in aid of its development; but in all that is done, it should not be forgotten, that even from its earliest infancy, it possesses a character and a principle of freedom, which *should be* respected, and *cannot* be destroyed. Its peculiar propensities may be discerned, and proper nutriment and culture supplied; but the infant plant, not less than the aged tree, must be permitted, with its own organs of absorption, to separate that which is peculiarly adapted to itself; otherwise it will be cast off as a foreign substance, or produce nothing but rottenness and deformity.

The science of the mind itself will be the effect of its own development. This is merely an attendant consciousness, which the mind possesses, of the growth of its own powers; and therefore, it would seem, need not be made a distinct object of study. Thus the power of reason may be imperceptibly developed by the study of the demonstrative sciences. As it is developed, the pupil becomes conscious of its existence and its use. This is enough. He can in fact learn nothing more on the subject. If he learns to use his reason, what more is desired? Surely it were useless, and worse than useless, to shut up the door of the senses, and live in indolent and laborious contemplation of one's own powers; when, if anything is learned truly, it must be what these powers are, and therefore that they ought not to be thus employed. The best affections we possess will find their home in the objects around us, and, as it were, enter into and animate the whole rational, animal, and vegetable world. If the eye were turned inward to a direct contemplation of these affections, it would find them bereft of all their loveliness; for when they are active, it is not of them we are thinking, but of the objects on which they rest. The science of the mind, then, will be the effect of all the other sciences. Can the child grow up in active usefulness, and not be conscious of the possession and use of his own limbs? The body and the mind should grow together, and form the sound and perfect man, whose understanding may be almost measured by his stature. The mind will see itself in what it loves and is able to accomplish. Its own works will be its mirror; and when it is present in the natural world, feeling the same spirit which gives life to every object by which it is surrounded, in its very union with nature it will catch a glimpse of itself, like that of pristine beauty united with innocence, at her own native fountain.

What then is that development which the nature of the human mind requires? What is that education which has heaven for its object, and such a heaven as will be the effect of the orderly growth of the spiritual man?

As all minds possess that in common which makes them human, they require to a certain extent the same general development, by which will be brought to view the same powers, however distinct and varied they may be found in different individuals; and as every mind possesses something peculiar, to which it owes its character and its effect, it requires a particular development by which may be produced a full, sincere, and humble expression of its natural features, and the most vigorous and efficient exertion of its natural powers. These make one, so far as regards the individual.

Those sciences which exist embodied in the natural world, appear to have been designed to occupy the first place in the development of all minds, or in that which might be called the general development of the mind. These comprise the laws of the animal, vegetable and mineral kingdoms. The human mind, being as it were planted in nature by its heavenly Father, was designed to enter into matter, and detect knowledge, for its own purposes of growth and nutrition. This gives us a true idea of memory, or rather of what memory should be. We no longer think of a truth as being laid up in a mind for which it has no affinity, and by which it is perhaps never to be used; but the latent affections, as they expand under proper culture, absolutely require the truth to receive them, and its first use is the very nutriment it affords. It is not more difficult for the tree to return to the seed from which it sprung, than for the man who has learned thus, to cease to remember. The natural sciences are the basis of all useful knowledge, alike important to man in whatever time, place or condition he is found. They are coeval with our race, and must continue so long as the sun, moon and stars endure. Before there were facts for the pen of history to record, or vices for the arm of law to restrain, or nations for the exhibition of institutions for the government of themselves and intercourse with each other, at the very creation, these were pronounced good in the general benediction; and when history shall have finished her tale of sin and woe, and law shall have punished her millions of offenders, and civil society shall have assumed every possible form, they will remain the same as when presented in living characters to the first parents of the human race.

Natural philosophy seems almost essential to an enlightened independence of thought and action. A man may lean upon others, and be so well supported by an equal pressure in all directions, as to be apparently dependent on no one; but his independence is apt to degenerate into obstinacy, or betray itself in weakness, unless his mind is fixed on this unchanging basis. A knowledge of the world may give currency to his sentiments, and plausibility to his manners; but it is more frequently a knowledge of *the world* that gives light to the path, and stability to the purposes. By the one he may learn what coin is current, by the other what possesses intrinsic value. The natural world was precisely and perfectly adapted to invigorate and strengthen the intellectual and moral man. Its first and highest use was not to support the vegetables which adorn, or the animals which cover, its surface; nor yet to give sustenance to the human body;—it has a higher and holier object, in the attainment of which these are only means. It was intended to draw forth and mature the latent energies of the soul; to impart to them its own verdure and freshness; to initiate them into its own mysteries; and by its silent and humble dependence on its Creator, to leave on them, when it is withdrawn by death, the full impression of his likeness.

It was the design of Providence, that the infant mind should possess the germ of every science. If it were not so, they could hardly be learned. The care of God provides for the flower of the field a place wherein it may grow, regale with its fragrance, and delight with its beauty. Is his providence less active over those to whom this flower offers its incense? No. The soil which produces the vine in its most healthy luxuriance is not better adapted to the end, than the world we inhabit to draw forth the latent energies of the soul, and fill them with life and vigor. As well might the eye see without light, or the ear hear without sound, as the human mind be healthy and athletic without descending into the natural world and breathing the mountain air. Is there aught in eloquence, which warms the heart? She draws her fire from natural imagery. Is there aught in poetry to enliven the imagination? There is the secret of all her power. Is there aught in science to add strength and dignity to the human mind? The natural world is only the body, of which she is the soul. In books science is presented to the eye of the pupil, as it were in a dried and preserved state; the time may come when the instructer will take him by the hand, and lead him by the running streams, and teach him all the principles of science as she comes from her Maker, as he would smell the fragrance of the rose without gathering it.

This love of nature, this adaptation of man to the place assigned him by his heavenly Father, this fulness of the mind as it descends into the works of God, is something which has been felt by every one, though to an imperfect degree; and therefore needs no explanation. It is the part of science, that this be no longer a blind affection; but that the mind be opened to a just perception of what it is which it loves. The affection which the lover first feels for his future wife, may be attended only by a general sense of her external beauty; but his mind gradually opens to a perception of the peculiar features of the soul, of which the external appearance is only an image. So it is with nature. Do we love to gaze on the sun, the moon, the stars, and the planets? This affection contains in its bosom the whole science of astronomy, as the seed contains the future tree. It is the office of the instructer to give it an existence and a name, by making known the laws which govern the motions of the heavenly bodies, the relation of these bodies to each other, and their uses. Have we felt delight in beholding the animal creation, in watching their pastimes and their labors? It is the office of the instructer to give birth to this affection, by teaching the different classes of animals, with their peculiar characteristics, which inhabit the earth, air and sea. Have we known the inexpressible pleasure of beholding the beauties of the vegetable world? This affection can only expand in the science of botany. Thus it is that the love of nature in the mass, may become the love of all the sciences, and the mind will grow and bring forth fruit from its own inherent power of development. Thus it is that memory refers to the growth and expansion of the mind; and what is thus, as it were, incorporated into its substance, can be forgotten only by a change in the direction of the affections, or the course of conduct of the individual analogous to that in his physical man, by which his very flesh and bones are exchanged for those of a different texture; nor does he then entirely cease to remember, inasmuch as he preserves a sense of his own identity.

It is in this way the continual endeavor of Providence, that the natural sciences should be the spontaneous production of the human mind. To these should certainly be added, poetry and music; for when we study the works of God as we should, we cannot disregard that inherent beauty and harmony in which these arts originate. These occasion in the mind its first glow of delight, like the taste of food, as it is offered to the mouth; and the pleasure they afford, is a pledge of the strength and manhood afterwards imparted by the sciences.

By poetry is meant all those illustrations of truth by natural imagery, which spring from the fact, that this world is the mirror of Him who made it. Strictly speaking, nothing has less to do with fiction than poetry. The day will come, and it may not be far distant, when this art will have another test of merit than mere versification, or the invention of strange stories; when the laws by which poetry is tested will be as fixed and immutable as the laws of science; when a change will be introduced into taste corresponding to that which Bacon introduced into philosophy, by which both will be confined within the limits of things as they actually exist. It would seem that genius would be cramped; that the powers of invention would be destroyed; by confining the human mind, as it were, at home, within the bounds which nature has assigned. But what wider scope need it have? It reaches the throne of God; it rests on his footstool. All things spiritual and natural are before it. There is as much that is true as false; and truth presented in natural imagery, is only dressed in the garments which God has given it.

The imagination was permitted for ages to involve the world in darkness, by putting theory in the place of fact; till at length the greatest man revealed the simplest truth, that our researches must be governed by actual observation. God is the source of all truth. Creation (and what truth does not result from creation?) is the effect of the Divine Love and Wisdom. Simply to will and to think, with the Divine Being, result in creating; in actually producing those realities, which form the groundwork of the thoughts and affections of man. But for the philosopher to desire a thing, and to think that it existed, produced nothing but his own theory. Hence it was necessary that he should bring his mind into coincidence with things as they exist, or, in other words, with the truth.

Fiction in poetry must fall with theory in science, for they depend equally on the works of creation. The word fiction, however, is not intended to be used in its most literal sense; but to embrace whatever is not in exact agreement with the creative spirit of God. It belongs to the true poet to feel this spirit, and to be governed by it; to be raised above the senses; to live and breathe in the inward efforts of things; to feel the power of creation, even before he sees the effect; to witness the innocence and smiles of nature's infancy, not by extending the imagination back to chaos, but by raising the soul to nature's origin. The true poetic spirit, so far from misleading any, is the strongest bulwark against deception. It is the soul of science. Without it, the latter is a cheerless, heartless study, distrusting even the presence and power of Him to whom it owes its existence. Of all the poetry which exists, that only possesses the seal of immortality, which presents the image of God which is stamped on nature. Could the poetry which now prevails be viewed from the future, when all partialities and antipathies shall have passed away, and things are left to rest on their own foundations; when good works shall have dwindled into insignificance, from the mass of useless matter that may have fallen from them, and bad ones shall have ceased to allure with false beauty; we might catch a glimpse of the rudiments of this divine art, amid the weight of extraneous matter by which it is now protected, and which it is destined to throw off. The imagination will be refined into a chaste and sober view of unveiled nature. It will be confined within the bounds of reality. It will no longer lead the way to insanity and madness, by transcending the works of creation, and, as it were, wandering where God has no power to protect it; but finding a resting-place in every created object, it will enter into it and explore its hidden treasures, the relation in which it stands to mind, and reveal the love it bears to its Creator.

The state of poetry has always indicated the state of science and religion. The gods are hardly missed more, when removed from the temples of the ancients, than they are when taken from their poetry; or than theory is when taken from their philosophy. Fiction ceases to be pleasing when it ceases to gain credence; and what they admired in itself, commands much of its admiration now, as a relic of antiquity. The painting which in a darkened room only impressed us with the reality, as the sun rises upon it discovers the marks of the pencil; and that shade of the mind can never again return, which gave to ancient poetry its vividness and its power. Of this we may be sensible, by only considering how entirely powerless it would be, if poetry in all respects similar were produced at the present day. A man's religious sentiments, and his knowledge of the sciences, are so entirely interwoven with all his associations; they shed such light throughout every region of the mind; that nothing can please which is directly opposed to them;—and though the forms which poetry may offer may sometimes be presented where this light begins to sink into obscurity, they should serve, like the sky and the clouds, as a relief to the eye, and not, like some unnatural body protruding on the horizon, disturb the quiet they are intended to produce. When there shall be a religion which shall see God in every thing, and at all times; and the natural sciences, not less than nature itself, shall be regarded in connection with Him; the fire of poetry will begin to be kindled in its immortal part, and will burn without consuming. The inspiration so often feigned, will become real, and the mind of the poet will feel the spark which passes from God to nature. The veil will be withdrawn, and beauty and innocence displayed to the eye; for which the lasciviousness of the imagination and the wantonness of desire may seek in vain.

There is a language, not of words, but of things. When this language shall have been made apparent, that which is human will have answered its end; and being as it were resolved into its original elements, will lose itself in nature. The use of language is the expression of our feelings and desires—the manifestation of the mind. But everything which is, whether animal or vegetable, is full of the expression of that use for which it is designed, as of its own existence. If we did but understand its language, what could our words add to its meaning? It is because we are unwilling to hear, that we find it necessary to say so much; and we drown the voice of nature with the discordant jargon of ten thousand dialects. Let a man's language be confined to the expression of that which actually belongs to his own mind; and let him respect the smallest blade which grows, and permit it to speak for itself. Then may there be poetry, which may not be written perhaps, but which may be felt as a part of our being. Everything which surrounds us is full of the utterance of one word, completely expressive of its nature. This word is its name; for God, even now, could we but see it, is creating all things, and giving a name to every work of his love, in its perfect adaptation to that for which it is designed. But man has abused his power, and has become insensible to the real character of the brute creation; still more so to that of inanimate nature, because, in his selfishness, he is disposed to reduce them to slavery. Therefore he is deaf. We find the animal world either in a state of savage wildness, or enslaved submission. It is possible, that, as the character of man is changed, they may attain a midway condition equally removed from both. As the mind of man acknowledges its dependence on the Divine Mind, brutes may add to their instinct submission to human reason; preserving an unbroken chain from our Father in Heaven, to the most inanimate parts of creation. Such may be supposed to have been the condition of the animal on which the King of Zion rode into Jerusalem; at once free and subject to the will of the rider. Everything will seem to be conscious of its use; and man will become conscious of the use of everything.

It may be peculiar, and is said with deference to the opinions of others, but to my ear, rhymes add nothing to poetry, but rather detract from its beauty. They possess too strongly the marks of art; and produce a sameness which tires, and sometimes disgusts. We seek for them in vain in nature, and may therefore reasonably presume that they spring out of the peculiar state of the public taste, without possessing any real foundation in the mind itself; that they are rather the fashion of the dress than any essential part. In the natural world we find nothing which answers to them, or feels like them, but a happy assemblage of living objects springing up, not in straight lines and at a fixed distance, but in God's own order, which by its apparent want of design, conveys the impression of perfect innocence and humility. It is not for that which is human to be completely divested of the marks of art; but every approach towards this end, must be an approach towards perfection. The poet should be free and unshackled as the eagle; whose wings, as he soars in the air, seem merely to serve the office of a helm, while he moves on simply by the agency of the will.

By music is meant not merely that which exists in the rational world, whether in the song of angels or men; not merely the singing of birds and the lowing of cattle, by which the animal world express their affections and their wants—but that harmony which pervades also all orders of creation; the music of the harp of universal nature, which is touched by the rays of the sun, and whose song is the morning, the evening and the seasons. Music is the voice of God, and poetry his language, both in his Word and works. The one is to the ear, what the other is to the eye. Every child of nature must feel their influence. There was a time, when the human mind was in more perfect harmony with the Divine Mind, than the lower orders of creation; and the tale of the harp of Orpheus, to which the brutes, the vegetables, and the rocks listened, is not altogether unfounded in reality; but when the selfish and worldly passions usurped the place of love to our God and our neighbor, the mind of man began to be mute in its praise. The original order was reversed. The very stones cry out, and we do well to listen to them.

There is a most intimate and almost inseparable connection between poetry and music. This is indicated by the fact that they are always united. Nothing is sung which has not some pretensions to poetry; and nothing has any pretensions to poetry in which there is not something of music. A good ear is essential to rhythm; and rhythm is essential to verse. It is the perfection of poetry, that it addresses two senses at once, the ear and the eye; that it prepares the affections for the object before it is presented; that it sends light through the understanding, by forming a communication between the heart of man and the works of God. The character of music must have always harmonized with that of poetry. It is essential to the former that it should be in agreement with our feelings; for it is from this circumstance that it derives its power. That music which is in unison with the Divine Mind, alone deserves the name. So various is it found in the different conditions of man, that it is hardly recognized as the same thing. There is music in the war-song of the savage, and in the sound for battle. Alas! how unlike that music, which proclaimed peace on earth and good will towards men. Poetry and music, like virtuous females in disguise, have followed our race into the darkest scenes to which the fall has brought them. We find them in the haunts of dissipation and vice; in the song of revelry and lewdness. We meet them again, kindling the fire of devotion at the altar of God; and find them more and more perfect as we approach their divine origin.

There prevail at present two kinds of music, as diverse as their origins—profane and religious. The one is the result of the free, unrestrained expression of natural feelings; the other, of a kind which indicates that these feelings are placed under restraint. In the one, there is often something of sensuality; in the other, of sadness. There is a point in moral improvement, in which the sensual will be subdued, and the sorrowful disappear; which will combine the pleasure of the one, with the sanctity of the other. When a sense of the presence of God shall be co-extensive with the thoughts of the mind, and religion shall consecrate every word and action of our lives, the song of Zion will be no longer sung in a strange land. The Divine Love, the soul and essence of music, will descend, not in the thunders of Sinai, but will seem to acquire volume, as it tunes the heart in unison with itself, and the tongue in unison with the heart. The changes in the character of our music, which may be the effect of the gradual regeneration of the world, are hardly within the reach of conjecture.

Enough has been said to illustrate generally the influence of the natural world in the development of the mind. The actual condition of society operates to produce the same effect, with hardly less power. In this are comprised the religious and civil institutions of one's own country; that peculiar character in which they originate; and a knowledge of the past, as, by disclosing the origin and progress of things, it throws light on the prospect actually before us. As the philosophy connected with the natural world is that in which the mind may take root, by which it may possess an independence worthy a being whose eternal destiny is in his own hands—so the moral and civil institutions, the actual condition of society, is the atmosphere which surrounds and protects it; in which it sends forth its branches, and bears fruit. The spiritual part of man is as really a substance, as the material; and is as capable of acting upon spirit, as matter is upon matter. It is not from words of instruction and advice, that the mind of the infant derives its first impetus; it gathers strength from the warmth of those affections which overshadow it, and is nourished by a mother's love, even before it has attained the power of thought. It is the natural tendency of things, that an individual should be brought into a situation, in which the external condition of the place, and the circle of society in which he is, are particularly adapted to bring forth to view his hereditary character. The actual condition of the human mind is, as it were, the solid substance, in which the laws of moral and intellectual philosophy and political economy (whatever may be their quality) exist embodied, as the natural sciences do in the material world. A knowledge of those laws, such as they exist, is the natural consequence of the development of the affections by which a child is connected with those that surround him. The connection of mind is not less powerful or universal than that of matter. All minds, whatever may be their condition, are not unconnected with God; and, consequently, not unconnected with each other. All nations, under whatever system of government, and in whatever state of civilization, are under the Divine Providence surely, but almost imperceptibly, advancing to a moral and political order, such as the world has not yet seen. They are guided by the same hand, and with a view to the same destiny.

Much remains to be done, and more to be suffered; but the end is certain. The humblest individual may, nay, *must*, aid in the accomplishment of this consummation. It is not for time or space to set limits to the effects of the life of a single man. Let then the child be so initiated into a knowledge of the condition of mankind, that the love at first indulged in the circle of his father's family shall gradually subside into a chaste and sober love of his country; and of his country, not as opposed to other countries, but as aiding them in the same great object. Let the young mind be warmed and cherished by whatever is chaste and generous in the mind of the public; and be borne on to a knowledge of our institutions, by the rich current of the disposition to preserve them.

Thus it is that the child is no sooner brought into this world, than the actual condition, both of the world itself, and of society, acts powerfully to draw forth the energies of his mind. If mankind had retained that order in which they were created, this influence, in co-operation with the Divine, would have been sufficient, as it was designed to have been, for all the purposes of God. Nature, the very image of divine loveliness, and the purest affections of the heart, which approach still nearer the same origin, acting together on the infant mind; it would seem as if the effect would be almost as certain as any process of growth which is witnessed among the productions of the natural world. But man is fallen; and the operation of this influence, in different conditions of society, may produce different results; but in none is sufficient to capacitate him for that life of usefulness and happiness, for which he was designed. The influence of society cannot be sufficient, since this cannot raise a man above its own level; and the society of earth is no longer the society of heaven. This influence may bring forward all the warlike energies of the young savage, and direct them in their utmost vigor to the destruction of his enemies and of the beasts of the forest; and he may look onward with rapture to the happy hunting grounds beyond the grave. What disappointment awaits him in the other world, all of us may easily imagine. This influence may bring forth and gratify the unchaste and beastly passions of the Turk; and he may look forward, with his Koran in his hand, to a heaven of sensuality and crime. It need not be said how widely different will be found the reality. Christians generally are standing in expectation of a happiness as boundless in extent, as it is undefined in its nature; and with an infinite variety of passions, in whose gratification alone they have experienced delight, are expecting a heaven in which simple useless enjoyment will rise like a flood and immerse the mind. The result must, of necessity, be as various as the condition of the individuals by whom it is anticipated. Still there is a society yet in its coming, unseen though not unseeing, shrouded from the rest of the world by the very brilliancy of its own light, which would resist the impulse of every evil affection, and look for heaven simply in the delight of that which is chaste, pure, and holy; which, by removing that which renders duty undelightful, would draw nigh to the only Source of real enjoyment; which would find its happiness and its God in the very commandments which have been the terror of the world; to which the effect is no longer doubtful, since it is made acquainted with the cause, and which, as it anticipates no reward, will meet with no disappointment. When this society shall be fully established on the earth, the voice of the Lord will be no longer obstructed as it descends from above the heavens; —"*Suffer little children to come unto me and forbid them not, for of such is the kingdom of God.*"

The influence of the natural world, however beneficial it may prove, is not such as it was designed to have been. Man has ever sought a condition in nature, which should correspond with the state of his own mind. The savage would pine and droop, if too suddenly removed to scenes of civilization, like grass which had grown in rank luxuriance under the shade of the oak, if the branches were cleft, and it was at once exposed to the power of the sun. The character of all the lower orders of creation has suffered a change in consequence of that in the condition of man, the extent of which cannot be measured. That the sun was darkened at the crucifixion of our Lord, was no miracle. It was as much the natural consequence of that event, as its present lustre is of His glory. It is not then for these, the objects of nature, to restore to us that moral order, the want of which has wrought such changes on themselves.

There is then another power which is necessary to the orderly development of the mind—the power of the Word of God. This indeed has been implied in all the preceding remarks. No possessions and no efforts of the mind are unconnected with it, whatever may be the appearance. Revelation so mingles with everything which meets us, that it is not easy for us to measure the degree to which our condition is affected by it. Its effects appear miraculous at first, but after they have become established, the mind, as in the ordinary operations of nature, is apt to become unconscious of the power by which they are produced. All growth or development is effected from within, outward. It is so with animals; it is so with vegetables; it is so with the body; it is so with the mind. Were it not for a power within the soul, as the soul is within the body, it could have no possibility of subsistence. That the growth of the material part depends on the presence of that which is spiritual, is obvious from the fact, that at death the former falls to decay. If it were possible for God to be detached from our spiritual part, this would decay likewise. The doctrine, then, of the immortality of the soul is, simply, "I in my Father, and ye in me, and I in you." It is the union of the Divine with the human—of that from which all things are, and on which they depend, the Divine Will, with man through the connecting medium of Divine Truth. It is the tendency of the Bible to effect this union, and of course to restore a consciousness of it. It is a union which God desires with all, therefore even the wicked who reject it partake of his immortality, though not of his happiness. When, in the process of regeneration, this union is accomplished, the fear of dissolution will be as impossible in this world as in the other; and before this is effected, the fear of dissolution may exist there as well as here. It is not the place where a person is, but the condition of mind, which is to be regarded; and there is no antidote against the fear of death, but the consciousness of being united with the Fountain of life. But it is asked, how can the fear of death exist after it has actually taken place? The separation of the spiritual and material part, so far as the nature of their connection is understood, can produce no fear. Were it not for evil in ourselves, it would rather wear the appearance of a state of uncommon quiet. There is upon no subject a more powerful tendency to instinctive knowledge, than upon that of death. The darkness with which it is veiled, presents but a lamentable picture of our present condition. It is its own dissolution of which the mind is afraid; and that want of conjunction with God which renders this fear possible here, may render it possible anywhere. It is the sole object of the Bible to conjoin the soul with God; and, as this is effected, it may be understood in what way the Holy Spirit operates interiorly to produce its development. It is not a mere metaphor, it is a plain and simple fact, that the Spirit of God is as necessary to the development of the mind, as the power of the natural sun to the growth of vegetables, and in the same way. But let us remember, that, as in nature the heat and light may be converted into the most noxious poison; so the Spirit of God, in itself perfectly pure and holy, may be converted into passions the most opposite to its nature. It is left to us to open our hearts to its influence, by obeying the commandments. "If ye love me, keep my commandments; and I will pray the Father, and he shall give you another Comforter that he may abide with you forever." "He that believeth on the Son *hath* everlasting life;" and he will become conscious of living and growing from God.

It is not consistent with the nature of things that the full practical effect of a subject should be at once revealed to the mind. The child is led on to a knowledge of his letters by a thousand little enticements, and by the tender coercion of parental authority, while he is yet ignorant of the treasures mysteriously concealed in their combinations. The arts have been courted merely for the transient gratification they afford. Their connection with religion and with the sciences is beginning to be discovered; and they are yet to yield a powerfûl influence in imparting to the mind its moral harmony and proportions. The sciences themselves have been studied principally as subjects of speculation and amusement. They have been sought for the gratification they afford, and for the artificial standing they give in society, by the line of distinction which is drawn between the learned and the vulgar. The discovery of their connection with the actual condition of man, is of later origin; and though their application to use is yet in its infancy, they are beginning to throw a light on almost every department of labor, hitherto unexampled in the annals of the world. Religion, too, has been a subject of speculation, something evanescent, a theory, a prayer, a hope. It remains for this also to become practical, by the actual accomplishment of that which it promises. It remains for the promise of reward to be swallowed up in the work of salvation. It remains for the soul to be restored to its union with God —to heaven. Christianity is the tree of life again planted in the world; and, by its own vital power, it has been, year after year, casting off the opinions of men, like the external bark which partakes not of its life. It remains for the human mind to become conformed to its spirit, that its principles may possess the durability of their origin.

Such are the effects to be anticipated from the Bible in the development of the mind. It has begun the work, and will perfect it in each individual, so far as, by a life according to the commandments, he becomes willing that it should. There is within it a secret power, which exerts an influence on the moral and intellectual world, like that of the sun on the physical; and, however long and successfully it may be resisted by some, not the less certain in its effect on the ultimate condition of society. I am aware that, in these remarks, I am ascribing to the spirit of God, to the spirit of the Word, a power which some may be unwilling to allow to it. The Bible is thought to resemble other books, and to be subject to the same laws of criticism; and we may be sometimes in danger of becoming insensible to its internal power, from the very mass of human learning with which it is encumbered. "Is not this the carpenter's son?"

There is one law of criticism, the most important to the thorough understanding of any work, which seems not to have been brought sufficiently into view in the study of the Bible. It is that by which we should be led by a continued exercise of those powers which are most clearly demonstrated in an author; by continued habits of mind and action; to approximate to that intellectual and moral condition, in which the work originated. If it were desired to make a child thoroughly acquainted with the work of a genuine poet, I would not put the poem and lexicon in his hand, and bid him study and learn—I would rather make him familiar with whatever was calculated to call forth the power of poetry in himself; since it requires the exercise of the same powers to understand, that it does to produce. I would point him to that source from which the author himself had caught his inspiration, and, as I led him to the baptismal fount of nature, I would consecrate his powers to that Being from whom nature exists. I would cultivate a sense of the constant presence and agency of God, and direct him inward to the presence-chamber of the Most High, that his mind might become imbued with His spirit. I would endeavor, by the whole course of his education, to make him a living poem, that, when he read the poetry of others, it might be effulgent with the light of his own mind. The poet stands on the mountain, with the face of nature before him, calm and placid. If we would enter into his views, we must go where he is. We must catch the direction of his eye, and yield ourselves up to the instinctive guidance of his will, that we may have a secret foretaste of his meaning —that we may be conscious of the image in its first conception—that we may perceive its beginnings and gradual growth, till at length it becomes distinctly depicted on the retina of the mind. Without this, we may take the dictionary in our hands and settle the definition of every word, and still know as little of the lofty conceptions of the author, as the weary traveller, who passes round in the farthest verge which is visible from the mountain, knows of the scenery which is seen from its summit. It has been truly said, that Johnson was incapable of conceiving the beauties of Milton. Yet Johnson was himself a living dictionary of Milton's language. The true poet, when his mind is full, fills his language to overflowing; and it is left to the reader to preserve what the words cannot contain. It is that part which cannot be defined; that which is too delicate to endure the unrestrained gaze; that which shrinks instinctively from the approach of anything less chaste than itself, and though present, like the inhabitants of the other world, is unperceived by flesh and blood, which is worth all the rest. This acknowledges no dwelling-place but the mind. Stamp the living light on the extended face of nature, beyond the power of darkness at the setting of the sun, and you may preserve such light as this, when the mind rises not to meet it in its coming.

If it were desired to make an individual acquainted with a work in one of the abstract sciences, this might be best effected by leading him gradually to whatever conduced to the growth of those powers, on which a knowledge of these sciences depends; by cultivating a principle of dependence on the Divine Being, a purity and chastity of the affections, which will produce a tranquil condition, of all things the most favorable to clear perceptions; by leading him to an habitual observation of the relations of things, and to such continued exertion of the understanding, as, calling into use its full powers without inducing fatigue, may impart the strength of the laborer, without the degradation of the slave; in a word, by forming a penetrating, mathematical mind, rather than by communicating mathematical information. The whole character and complexion of the mind will be gradually changed; till at length it will become, (chemically speaking) in its very nature, an active solvent of these subjects. They fall to pieces as soon as they come in contact with it, and assume an arrangement agreeable to that of the mind itself, with all the precision of crystallization. They are then understood; for the most perfect understanding of a subject is simply a perception of harmony existing between the subject and the mind itself. Indeed, the understanding which any individual possesses of a subject might be mathematically defined $\frac{\text{the subject proposed,}}{\text{the actual character of his mind}}$; and there is a constant struggle for the divisor and dividend to become the same by a change in the one or the other, that the result may be unity, and the understanding perfect.

There is an analogy, (such as may exist between things human and things divine,) between that discipline which is required in order to understand a production of taste or science, and that which is necessary to a clear perception of the truths of the Bible. As it is requisite to a full sense of the beauties of poetry, that the individual should be himself a poet, and to a thorough knowledge of a work of science, that he should not merely have scientific information, but a scientific mind; so it is necessary to a knowledge of the Bible, that the mind should be formed in the image and likeness of God. An understanding of the Word is the effect of a life according to its precepts. It requires, not the obedience of the rich man who went away sorrowful, but the obedience of him who holds every other possession, whether it consist in the acquirements of the mind or in earthly property, in subjection to the Holy Spirit within him. "If ye will do the will of God, ye shall know of the doctrine," is a law of exegesis, before which false sentiments will melt away, like frost before the rising sun. There is within the mind the golden vein of duty, which, if followed aright, will lead to an increasing brightness, before which the proudest monuments of human criticism will present an appearance like that of the dark disk of this world, as the eye of the dying man opens on the scenes of the other.

The world is beginning to be changed from what it was. Physical power, instead of boasting of its deeds of prowess, and pointing with the tomahawk or the lance to the bloody testimonies of its strength, is beginning to leave its image on the rugged face of nature, and to feel the living evidence of its achievements, in the happy circle of domestic life. It remains for intellectual strength to lose the consciousness of its existence in the passions subdued, and to reap the reward of its labors, not in the spoils of an enemy, but in the fruits of honest industry. It remains for us to become more thoroughly acquainted with the laws of moral mechanism. Instead of making unnecessary and ineffectual exertions in the direct attainment of truth, it remains for us to make equal efforts to cleanse our own minds and to do good to others; and what was before unattainable will become easy, as the rock which untutored strength cannot move, may be raised by a touch of the finger.

The Bible differs from other books, as our Lord differed from men. He was born of a woman, but His Spirit was the everlasting Father. It is humble in its appearance, as nature is when compared to art; and some parts which Providence has permitted to remain within the same cover have often attracted more attention than that which is really divine. From the very nature of perfect innocence its presence is unnoticed, save by him by whom it is loved. Divine Love, in its perfect thoughtlessness of itself, enters the atheistical heart, unperceived. Such an one thinks meanly of those who think humbly of themselves, and with perfect humility the last vestige of reality disappears. To him, both nature and the Word are like a deserted building, through which, as he passes, he is conscious of nothing but the sound of his own footsteps; but to him whose heart opens to the Divine Influence, this building appears to assume, from the internal cause of its creation, the symmetry of perfect proportions, till at length, as he becomes more and more conscious of the presence with which it is filled, he sees no temple, "for the Lord God Almighty and the Lamb are the temple." The Word resembles the Hebrew language, in which much of it is written. To him who knows not its spirit, it is an empty form without sound or vowel; but to him who is alive to the Divine Influence, it is filled with the living voice of God.

The Bible can never be fully understood, either by making it subservient to natural reason, or by blindly adopting what reason would reject; but by that illumination of the understanding and enlargement of the reason which will result from a gradual conformity to its precepts. Reason now is something very different from what it was a few centuries past. We are in the habit of thinking that the mode of reasoning has changed; but this appears to be merely an indication of a change which has taken place in the character of the mind itself. Syllogistic reasoning is passing away. It has left no permanent demonstration but that of its own worthlessness. It amounts to nothing but the discernment and expression of the particulars which go to comprise something more general; and, as the human mind permits things to assume a proper arrangement from their own inherent power of attraction, it is no longer necessary to bind them together with syllogisms. Few minds can now endure the tediousness of being led blindfold to a conclusion, and of being satisfied with the result merely from the recollection of having been satisfied on the way to it. The mind requires to view the parts of a subject, not only separately, but together; and the understanding, in the exercise of those powers of arrangement, by which a subject is presented in its just relations to other things, takes the name of reason. We appear to be approaching that condition which requires the union of reason and eloquence, and will be satisfied with neither without the other. We neither wish to see an anatomical plate of bare muscles, nor the gaudy daubings of finery; but a happy mixture of strength and beauty. We desire language neither extravagant nor cold, but blood-warm. Reason is beginning to learn the necessity of simply tracing the relations which exist between created things, and of not even touching what it examines, lest it disturb the arrangement in the cabinet of creation—and as, in the progress of moral improvement, the imagination (which is called the creative power of man) shall coincide with the actively creative will of God, reason will be clothed with eloquence, as nature is with verdure.

Reason is said to be a power given to man for his protection and safety. Let us not be deceived by words. If this were the particular design, it should be found in equal perfection in every condition of the mind; for all are in equal need of such a power. It is the office of the eye to discern the objects of nature, and it may protect the body from any impending injury; and the understanding may be useful in a similar way to the spiritual man. Reason is partly a natural and partly an acquired power. The understanding is the eye, with simply the power of discerning the light; but reason is the eye, whose powers have been enlarged by exercise and experience, which measures the distance of objects, compares their magnitudes, discerns their colors, and selects and arranges them according to the relation they bear to each other. In the progress of moral improvement no power of the mind, or rather no mode of exercising the understanding, undergoes a more thorough and decisive change than this. It is like the change from chaos to creation; since it requires a similar exercise of the understanding in man to comprehend creation, to what it does in God to produce it; and every approach to Him, by bringing us nearer the origin of things, enables us to discover analogies in what was before chaotic. This is a change which it is the grand design of revelation to accomplish; reason should therefore come to revelation in the spirit of prayer, and not in that of judgment. Nothing can be more intimately and necessarily connected with the moral character of an individual than his rational powers, since it is his moral character which is the grand cause of that peculiar classification and arrangement which characterizes his mind; hence revelation, in changing the former, must change the latter also.

The insufficiency of reason to judge of the Bible, is obvious on the very face of revelation from its miracles. The laws of Divine Operation are perfectly uniform and harmonious; and a miracle is a particular instance of Divine Power, which, for want of a more interior and extended knowledge of the ways of God, appearing to stand alone, and to have been the result of an unusual exertion of the Divine Will, creates in the minds of men, what its name implies, a sensation of wonder. That there are miracles in the Bible, proves that there are laws of the Divine Operation and of the Divine Government, which are not embraced within the utmost limits of that classification and arrangement, which is the result of natural reason. While, therefore, human reason professes to be convinced of the reality of revelation from its miracles, let it humble itself before them. Let it bow itself to the earth, that it may be exalted to a more intimate acquaintance with these heavenly strangers. Let it follow the Lord in the regeneration, till the wonderful disappear in the paternal. Miracles are like angels who have sometimes been visible to men, who would much more willingly have introduced them to an acquaintance with the laws and society of heaven, than have filled them with fear and consternation. They are insulated examples of laws as boundless as the universe, and by the manner in which we are affected by them, prove how much we have to learn, and how utterly incompetent we are to judge of the ways of God, from that reason which is founded on our own limited and fallacious observation. The resurrection of our Lord must have been a very different miracle to the angels at the sepulchre, from what it was to Mary. They saw it from the other side of the grave, with a knowledge of the nature of that death which they had themselves experienced; she saw an insulated fact, not at all coincident with her views on the subject of which it was an illustration. They saw the use and design of that which had been accomplished; she saw the sepulchre and the linen clothes lying. As they gazed intensely at the same subject, the veil of heaven was withdrawn, and they beheld each other, face to face. She was filled with fear; they with love and compassion. If Mary were to persist in judging of this subject from her own reason; from a knowledge of those laws with which she was previously acquainted; how could her views ever become angelic? How could the dark cloud of admiration be ever filled with the rich light of the rising sun?

Man alone, of all created things, appears on his own account to want the full measure of his happiness; because he alone has left the order of his creation. He stands, even at the present period, half convinced of the reality of the future state. It is the design of revelation to restore to him that moral condition in which he will possess as necessarily the consciousness of immortality, as the brute does that of existence; for a consciousness of existence, together with that of union with God, is a consciousness of eternal life. Let us come to the Bible, then, with no hopes of arbitrary reward, and no fears of arbitrary punishment; but let us come to it, as to that which, if followed aright, will produce a condition of mind of which happiness will be the natural and necessary consequence.

It is often said that the Bible has nothing to do with metaphysics or the sciences. An individual, whatever be his condition, always retains, to a certain extent, a consciousness of his moral and intellectual character; and the more this character is exalted, the more minute and discriminating will be this consciousness. Who is it that formed the human mind, and who is here endeavoring to restore it to its true order? The Bible has the mind for its subject, that condition of mind which is heaven for its object, and the Father of mind for its author. Has it nothing to do with metaphysics? It has indeed nothing to do with that metaphysics which we shall leave with our bodies in the graves; but of that, which will shine with more and more brilliancy, as the passage is opened, not through distant regions of space, but through the secret part of our own souls to the presence of God, it is the very life and being. Can omniscience contemplate the happiness of the mind, without regard to its nature? Were we disposed to improve the condition of the savage, what course should we pursue? Should we not endeavor to change his habits of mind and body, by teaching him the arts of civilization, instructing him in the sciences, and gradually introducing him to that portion of social order which is here attained? And are not all these most intimately connected with our own condition of mind? Are they not merely the expression of its countenance? In the same way is it the endeavor of the Divine Mind in the Bible to restore all to his own image and likeness; and to say that the Bible has nothing to do with metaphysics, is to say that the present condition of the mind has nothing to do with what it should be, and that present metaphysics have nothing to do with religion. It is said that the Bible has nothing to do with the sciences. It is true that it does not teach them directly; but it is gradually unfolding a condition of mind, out of which the sciences will spring as naturally, as the leaves and blossoms from the tree that bears them. It is the same power which acts simultaneously to develop the soul itself, and to develop nature—to form the mind and the mould which is destined to receive it. As we behold the external face of the world, our souls will hold communion with its spirit; and we shall seem to extend our consciousness beyond the narrow limits of our own bodies, to the living objects that surround us. The mind will enter into nature by the secret path of him who forms her; and can be no longer ignorant of her laws, when it is a witness of her creation.

I have endeavored to illustrate, generally, in what way the natural sciences, the actual condition of society, and the Word of God, are necessary to the development of all minds, in a manner analogous to that in which the earth, the atmosphere and the sun combine to bring forth the productions of nature. I shall say but a few words with respect to that particular development which is requisite to the full manifestation of the peculiar powers possessed by any individual.

It is well known that at a certain period of life the character of a man begins to be more distinctly marked. He appears to become separated from that which surrounds him—to stand in a measure aloof from his associates—to raise his head above the shadow of any earthly object into the light of heaven, and to walk with a more determined step on the earth beneath. This is the manifestation of a character which has always existed, and which has, as it were, been accumulating by little and little, till at length it has attained its full stature.

When a man has become his own master, it is left to himself to complete his own education. "He has one Father, God." For the formation of his character, thus far, he is not in the strictest sense accountable; that is, his character is not as yet so fixed, but that it is yielding and pliable. It is left to himself to decide, how far it shall remain in its present form. This is indeed a period of deep responsibility. He has taken the guidance of a human being, and is not the less accountable, that this being is himself. The ligament is now cut asunder by which his mind was bound to its earthly guardian, and he is placed on his own feet, exposed to the bleak winds and refreshing breezes, the clouds and the sunshine of this world, fully accountable to God and man for his conduct. Let him not be made dizzy from a sense of his own liberty, nor faint under his own weight; but let him remember that the eye of God is now fixed full, it might almost be said anxiously, upon him.

It is with the human mind, as with the human body. All our race have those limbs and features, and that general aspect, from which they are denominated men. But, on a nearer view, we find them divided into nations possessed of peculiar appearance and habits, and these subdivided into families and individuals, in all of which there is something peculiarly their own. The human mind (speaking in the most general sense) requires to be instructed in the same sciences, and needs the same general development, and is destined to make one common and universal effort for its own emancipation. But the several nations of the earth also will, at a future period, stand forth with a distinctness of character which cannot now be conceived of. The part which each is to perform in the regeneration of the world, will become more and more distinctly marked and universally acknowledged; and every nation will be found to possess resources in its own moral and intellectual character, and its own natural productions, which will render it essential to the well-being and happiness of the whole. Every government must find that the real good of its own people precisely harmonizes with that of others; and standing armies must be converted into willing laborers for the promotion of the same object. Then will the nations of the earth resemble the well-organized parts of the same body, and no longer convert that light which is given them for the benefit of their brethren, into an instrument by which they are degraded and enslaved.

But we stop not here. Every individual also possesses peculiar powers, which should be brought to bear on society in the duties best fitted to receive them. The highest degree of cultivation of which the mind of any one is capable, consists in the most perfect development of that peculiar organization, which as really exists in infancy as in maturer years. The seed which is planted is said to possess in miniature, the trunk, branches, leaves and fruit of the future tree. So it is with the mind; and the most that can possibly be done, is to afford facilities by which its development may be effected with the same order. In the process of the formation of our minds there exists the spirit of prophecy; and no advancement can create surprise, because we have always been conscious of that from which it is produced. We must not seek to make one hair white or black. It is in vain for us to attempt to add one cubit to our stature. All adventitious or assumed importance should be cast off, as a filthy garment. We should seek an employment for the mind, in which all its energies may be warmed into existence; which (if I may be allowed the expression) may bring every muscle into action. There is something which every one can do better than any one else; and it is the tendency, and must be the end, of human events, to assign to each his true calling. Kings will be hurled from their thrones, and peasants exalted to the highest stations, by this irresistible tendency of mind to its true level. These effects may not be fully disclosed in the short period of this life; but even the most incredulous must be ultimately convinced that the truth is no respecter of persons, by learning the simple fact, that a man cannot be other than what he is. Not that endless progression in moral goodness and in wisdom are not within the reach of any one; but that the state will never arrive, when he may not look back to the first rudiments, the original stamina of his own mind, and be almost able to say, I possessed all at the time of my birth. The more a person lives in singleness of heart, in simplicity, and sincerity, the more will this be apparent.

It becomes us, then, to seek and to cherish this *peculium* of our own minds, as the patrimony which is left us by our Father in heaven—as that by which the branch is united to the vine—as the forming power within us, which gives to our persons that by which they are distinguished from others; and, by a life entirely governed by the commandments of God, to leave on the duties we are called to perform the full impress of our real characters. Let a man's ambition to be great disappear in a willingness to be what he is; then may he fill a high place without pride, or a low one without dejection. As our desires become more and more concentrated to those objects which correspond to the peculiar organization of our minds, we shall have a foretaste of that which is coming, in those internal tendencies of which we are conscious. As we perform with alacrity whatever duty presents itself before us, we shall perceive in our own hearts a kind of preparation for every external event or occurrence of our lives, even the most trivial, springing from the all-pervading tendency of the Providence of God, to present the opportunity of being useful wherever there is the disposition.

Living in a country whose peculiar characteristic is said to be a love of equal liberty, let it be written on our hearts, that the end of all education is a life of active usefulness. We want no education which shall raise a man out of the reach of the understanding, or the sympathies of any of his species. We are disgusted with that kind of dignity which the possessor is himself obliged to guard; but venerate that, which, having its origin in the actual character of the man, can receive no increase from the countenance of power, and suffer no diminution from the approach of weakness —that dignity in which the individual appears to live rather in the consciousness of the light which shines from above, than in that of his own shadow beneath. There is a spiritual atmosphere about such an one, which is at once its own protection, and the protection of him with whom it is connected—which, while it is free as air alike to the most powerful and the most humble, conveys a tacit warning that too near an approach is not permitted. We acknowledge the invisible chain which binds together all classes of society, and would apply to it the electric spark of knowledge with the hand of tenderness and caution. We acknowledge the healthy union of mental and bodily exercise, and would rather see all men industrious and enlightened, than to see one half of mankind slaves to the other, and these slaves to their passions. We acknowledge that the natural world is one vast mine of wisdom, and for this reason it is the scene of the labors of man; and that in seeing this wisdom, there is philosophy, and in loving it, there is religion. Most sensibly do we feel, that as the true end of instruction is to prepare a man for some particular sphere of usefulness; that when he has found this sphere, his education has then truly commenced, and the finger of God is pointing to the very page of the book of his oracles, from which he may draw the profoundest wisdom. It was the design of Providence that there should be enough of science connected with the calling of each for the highest and holiest purposes of heaven. It is the natural world from which the philosopher draws his knowledge; it is the natural world in which the slave toils for his bread. Alas! when will they be one? When we are willing to practise what we learn, and religion makes our duty our delight. The mass of mankind must always labor; hence it is supposed that they must be always ignorant. Thus has the pride of man converted that discipline into an occasion of darkness and misery, which was intended only to give reality to knowledge, and to make happiness eternal. Truth is the way in which we should act; and then only is a man truly wise when the body performs what the mind perceives. In this way, flesh and blood are made to partake of the wisdom of the spiritual man; and the palms of our hands will become the book of our life, on which is inscribed all the love and all the wisdom we possess. It is the light which directs a man to his duty; it is by doing his duty that he is enlightened—thus does he become identified with his own acts of usefulness, and his own vocation is the silken chord which directs to his heart the knowledge and the blessings of all mankind.

SELECTIONS

FROM THE

NEW JERUSALEM MAGAZINE.

The following articles, having more or less bearing on subjects which have been touched upon in the preceding pages, are added. They were first published in the New Jerusalem Magazine.

SELECTIONS.

MIRACLES.

The most ancient church, represented by Adam, enjoyed an uninterrupted intercourse with the spiritual world. Inhabitants at once of the spiritual world and the natural, and conscious of their union with God, their residence on earth was simply the commencement of that course of life, in the progress of which, according to the divine order, at a certain period their internals divested themselves of that which was earthly, and they became as the angels of heaven. In the development of their powers there was nothing of violence; and death was regarded as a necessary consequence of this development. They were conscious of the presence of a divine power working within them, unloosing the chords which would confine them to a stifled sense of the use for which they were created, and pushing them on to a full and perfect evolution. Instead of shuddering at the thought of annihilation and a new creation, they attained to such a clear perception of the inward endeavors of the soul, that no longer fearing death, they actually co-operated with the Lord in this great event of their spiritual progress. They were not afraid to die; for they were not afraid to be more fully what they were already. Like a child, who has not yet left his father's house, they were strangers to the ills and the fears which have attended the wanderings of their posterity.

In process of time, this church degenerated. The love of self and of the world took the place of the love of the Lord and the neighbor; and a knowledge of the means to obtain selfish and worldly ends was substituted for a knowledge of the laws of divine order and of the things of the spiritual world. The communication of the Lord with man became necessarily miraculous; for the cause and the ground of miracles is to be found in the aversion of man to that which is concealed within the miracle. God remained, as he must, unchangeably the same; but man no longer continued to behold him in his works—in the order, the beauty, and the harmony of creation—because he had ceased to love him. As divine things became less and less familiar to the human mind, there was more and more a feeling of something strange and incongruous when they were presented. Mankind were as one who has been stolen in his childhood by a band of robbers, and made familiar to all their scenes of violence: to whom the recollections of his infancy appear like a strange dream, by which he is terrified far more than by crimes. It is a necessary consequence of the laws of divine order, that, to a certain extent, the absence of love should be supplied by fear. The Lord, however, so wonderfully veils His presence as to preserve the free-agency of man inviolate. The miraculous is the measure of our alienation from God; it represents the opposition of revealed truth to human depravity, and its want of coincidence with merely natural reason. There is something of the nature of a miracle in the relation between the Word of God and the human mind, precisely to that degree that we have not followed the Lord in the regeneration, and become conformed to His spirit. Miracles are not, strictly speaking, confined to those particular acts recorded in the Sacred Scripture, to which the term is usually applied. The whole Word is to the natural man a living miracle. "Unto us a child is born, unto us a son is given, and the government shall be upon his shoulder, and his name shall be called *wonderful*, counsellor, the mighty God, the everlasting Father, the Prince of peace."

As the conception and growth of the Lord was miraculous, so is there something wonderful in the commencement and progress of regeneration. Natural reason undergoes a complete inversion. In the exercise of reason, a subject is presented in such relations to others, with us of acknowledged truth, as to preserve the harmony, the order and the unity of the whole. Reason is the power of arrangement and organization; but that by which arrangement is effected, is always to be found within and above that which is arranged. In minerals, the cause of crystallization is to be found in the peculiar nature of a substance, which determines its particles to a particular form, in a manner altogether above the ordinary laws of attraction. In vegetables, the general form of the plant is wonderfully determined by the seed from which it is produced. In animals, the form and parts are precisely adapted to answer the end of that affection by which they are instinctively governed. In the human body, all the arrangement of the parts is effected from, and in relation to, one grand centre, the heart; and this, in its turn, acknowledges the supremacy of the brain; and the whole material man is precisely adapted to subserve the purposes of the soul, of which it is truly the effect. Thus, in all organized matter, there exists, as the cause of its organization, a power above the general laws by which matter is governed. The causes of decay and decomposition act equally while vegetable or animal life remains, as after it has ceased. But in the former case, these causes only co-operate with the life in removing the useless or noxious particles; that all which is without may be the servant of that which is within. The spiritual man is not exempted from this universal law. The actual cause of the arrangement of our thoughts, is to be found above the thoughts themselves, in that wherein they originate, the ruling love, or the will; and the understanding is considered the seat of reason, not because it creates this arrangement, but simply because it sees and points it out. A man's thoughts are arranged with a view to the accomplishment of his peculiar ends; and the character of his reason depends essentially on the fact whether these ends are good or bad; whether they regard self, or the Lord. Revelation, therefore, if obeyed, in gradually changing the ends from which we act, is undermining the very foundation of natural reason, by creating a new organization of our affections and thoughts. During this process, from our own want of conformity to the Word, it cannot but appear to us as something "wonderful."

The introduction of any new truth to the mind,

is like introducing a stranger into one's family, and giving him a situation and dress by which he becomes an acknowledged inmate, subject to the laws of the household. But if the master of the house discern, in this stranger, evidences of a character and of intelligence far above his own, the change that is effected is on his own part; his own understanding is enlightened; his own affections are exalted; his own manners are improved by the intercourse. If every moral and intellectual advancement he makes, only opens his eyes to the still more exalted character of the stranger, the influence on himself and his family will continue to be more and more visible. If finally he discern, in this stranger, the person of his rightful sovereign, who has laid aside the outward trappings of royalty, that his subjects might shew him simply the homage of the affections,—how will his heart burn within him as he recalls the scenes that have past; even from the time that he "was an hungered, and he gave him meat; was thirsty, and he gave him drink; a stranger, and he took him in."

There exist, at the present day, two prevailing opinions in respect to reason, to my apprehension equally at variance with the truth. By one class, the supremacy of natural reason is boldly asserted, and its entire competence to judge on matters of faith. By another class, faith and reason are kept entirely distinct, from a kind of implied acknowledgment that they cannot co-exist. They are unhappily involved in the same delusion, that there is no necessity of a change on their own part. The first falsify divine truth, by reducing it into harmony with the existing condition of their own minds; the last keep that which they call truth distinct from their minds, without suffering themselves to be transformed into its image. But "now also is the axe laid at the *root* of the trees; every tree, therefore, that bringeth not forth good fruit, is hewn down and cast into the fire." Nothing but obedience to the Word of God, from grounds more and more interior, can teach the former the extent of their presumption, folly and danger; or impart unity to the minds of the latter, by removing that which is irrational from their faith, and that which is immoral from their reason.

If we examine the general character of the miracles recorded in the Old and New Testaments, we shall be convinced that these partake fully of the peculiarities of the two dispensations. They were not a mere arbitrary exhibition of divine power, but the necessary result of the presence of divine truth, and consequently varied with the degree in which it was presented. There is really no more ground of surprise, that the Jews were not convinced by the miracles of our Lord, than that they misapplied the prophecies concerning him. Both proceeded from the same source, and both were separated, by their self-love, from the source from which they proceeded. The same cause which prevented their looking through the letter into the spirit of prophecy, prevented their looking beyond the exhibition of mere physical power, to the divine love and wisdom which produced it. Their language at the crucifixion, in that they called upon the Lord both for a prophecy and a miracle, is an illustration of their total insensibility to the spirit of both.

Who shall predict the character of the miracles which shall accompany a still further manifestation of divine truth? Who shall demand a thing impossible in itself, the same effects from the revelation of one order of truth, which have previously attended that of another? When "the veil of the temple was rent in twain, from the top to the bottom, and the earth did quake, and the rocks rent, and the graves were opened, and many bodies of saints which slept arose," the heavens were in a state of comparative quiet; and as we enter into the spirit of the Word, we draw nigh to the Lamb, but feel not his wrath. The clouds which overhang the earth, are seen from the other side, gilded with the light of heaven. The wonders of divine truth advance inward; they are displayed not on inanimate nature, nor yet on the human body,—but the natural mind becomes the scene of their exhibition. "Father, glorify thy name. Then came there a voice from heaven, I have both glorified, and will glorify again. The people, therefore, that stood by and heard, said that it thundered, others said that an angel spake to him. Jesus answered and said, this voice came not because of me, but for your sakes."

The world appears to be under a decidedly false impression, in regard to the design of miracles, in supposing them intended primarily as evidence of a divine mission. Their effect on the mind, in some states, in this respect, is merely an incidental circumstance. Miracles were not wrought by our Lord with this end; and in proportion as we take delight, that "the blind see, the lame walk, the lepers are cleansed, the deaf hear, the dead are raised, and to the poor the gospel is preached,"—we shall not make this use of them, any more than we shall look for a reward for the performance of our duty, when the act finds no opposition in our hearts. The miracles wrought by our Lord were not a momentary exhibition of power, which then ceased to operate, that the mind should find it necessary to go back to that period in order to realize its existence. The eternal fountain of divine love was opened.

The same power which removed blindness, raised the dead, cast out devils, now imparts vision and life, and delivers from evil; and the only true practical belief in those miracles, consists in a perception of this fact. "And when the tempter came to him, he said, If thou be the Son of God, command that these stones be made bread. But he answered and said, It is written, man shall not live by bread alone, but by every word that proceedeth out of the mouth of God. Then the devil taketh him up into the holy city, and setteth him on the pinnacle of the temple, and saith unto him, If thou be the Son of God, cast thyself down, for it is written, He shall give his angels charge concerning thee; and in their hands they shall bear thee up, lest at any time thou dash thy foot against a stone. Jesus said unto him, It is written again, thou shalt not tempt the Lord thy God."

But though the miracles, wrought by our Lord, were simply the operations of his divine love and wisdom, by which disorders, spiritual and natural, were cured,—it was not foreign from their purpose, that they should awaken the attention of those who were well disposed, but yet not in a state to be fellow-laborers with him—yet ignorant of the Father who doeth the works. When "John, calling two of his disciples, sent to Jesus, saying, art thou he that should come, or look we for another?"—He directed them to his works. By John and his disciples, are represented the literal sense of the Word, and those who are in good in that degree. There is no reason to doubt that miracles have been useful, in this way, to the Christian church. But those who have entered within the letter, and view our Lord's miracles from their true source, are carried by his spirit *into* the works, which those on the outside regard as some evidence of his existence. The natural world may afford, to the skeptical mind, grounds of belief in the existence of a God. Yet who would say that this was the design of its creation? It was created by the Lord that it might be the seminary of heaven; and though I would discourage no man from finding in it evidences of the divine existence, I am aware that this will be no longer necessary, when he becomes so united with the Lord, as to feel that his own existence, and that of nature, are alike constantly dependent upon Him.

It can never be too deeply impressed on the mind, that a miracle derives its specific character as such, not more from the nature of the act itself, than from the state of those by whom it is witnessed. There are no miracles connected with the revelation of the spiritual sense of the Sacred Scripture, because with those who receive it, religion can no longer be regarded as a prodigy or a monster. It no longer retains a secluded, insulated seat in their minds, approached from motives of fear or interest, and secretly held as a tyrant, or viewed with contempt. It becomes their constant daily meat and drink, assimilating all things of the man to itself, and clothing itself with flesh and blood, as with a garment. The very cause of miracles is removed. The spiritual truths of the Word are not only not dependent upon any new miracles for their support, but to those who follow them aright, that which is recorded as miraculous in the letter, ceases to appear such. They create a sense of the presence and agency of God as constant and uniform as the laws of nature, and felt more powerfully in the operation of these laws, than they ever could have been in their apparent interruption. The truths of the spiritual sense of the Sacred Scripture derive illustration and confirmation from whatever of beauty or harmony exists in the natural world, and can receive no new evidence from aught that would seem to disturb the ground on which they rest. Picture to the mind the astonished multitude which had just witnessed one of the miracles of our Lord—the effect of the spiritual sense of the Word may be justly represented, by the countenances of the beholders, receiving a gentle emanation of light from the divine Performer, which melts their fear and astonishment into an expression of subdued affection and exalted intelligence. When our Lord was upon earth, He descended into nature, and miracles were the necessary consequence. It remains for man to ascend into heaven; to become transformed into the image of those very works which have filled him with wonder. That part of the covenant which belongs to God, is fulfilled; that which depends on the reaction of man, remains to be accomplished. While the prodigal son is in a far country, wasting his substance, the messenger from his native land is a bearer of strange tidings; but when he has returned, all other feelings yield to the warmth of a father's love, and the tender remembrances of infancy and childhood. Those who ask for miracles as proof of the spiritual sense of the Sacred Scripture, truly ask an impossibility. All Christendom is acknowledging our Lord with their lips; when lo! He is standing in the midst of them, and they know Him not. We say, "if we had been in the days of our fathers, we would not have been partakers with them in the blood of the prophets;"—yet is the holy Word profaned; its divinity is denied, and its letter is made the subject of contention. "They parted my garments among them, and upon my vesture did they cast lots." The language with some, is now as it was then, "if thou be the Son of God come down from the cross."

It requires an extraordinary excitement, and an unusual exemption from the fear of the law, for the actual manifestation of those evils which really exist in the human heart;—yet is it a fact, that during the revolution in France, the Almighty was publicly defied to prove his existence by a miracle. Then, too, was merely natural reason worshipped in the person of her just representative, that of a prostitute. We say just representative, because it has always been, and must always continue to be, her degraded office, to afford grounds of belief, not in that which is true, but in that which favors the lusts of the natural man, of which she is the servant.

All that is violent in the divine operations appears to be occasioned by the want of proper mediums of the divine influx: as thunderings and lightnings, in the natural world, are produced by the want of conductors for the proper distribution of the electric fluid. All that is violent in the operation of chemical agents, is to be accounted for in a similar way. Substances are brought into contact which are constantly existing in and about us; but they exist in the most intimate relation to other substances, with which they are in amity, and all is peace and order. The lamp burns bright and quietly in the atmosphere, as God has formed it; but when it is confined to one of the component parts of this atmosphere, darkness or an overpowering brilliancy is the consequence. The spiritual world is not exempted from corresponding laws. Their operation is exemplified in the death of Uzzah, when he took hold of the ark. "And the anger of the Lord was kindled against Uzzah, and God smote him there for his error; and there he died by the ark of God." So also, when the commandments were given on Mount Sinai, "the Lord said unto Moses, go down, charge the people, lest they break through unto the Lord to gaze, and many of them perish." In the ark, and the commandments it contained, Jehovah was peculiarly present; and as the Jews could not acknowledge him in their hearts, they could not approach his presence with safety, excepting such as were miraculously prepared by means of external representatives. Analogous to these, is a fact mentioned by Swedenborg, in the spiritual world, of a violent explosion, when the Word was approached by one by whom it had been falsified. To a similar cause is to be ascribed the surprise attending the abrupt communication of an important truth, without having prepared the mind for its reception by the preliminary steps. The truth stands insulated—detached from its proper mediums. When the child is first told that the sun, moon and stars do not revolve round the earth, he is filled with astonishment; but when the comparative size and uses of these several bodies, with the immense distance they would have to pass, are explained, this astonishment ceases. When we see simply the fact that the dead were restored to life by our Lord, we cannot but marvel; but when we understand what life is, the connection of things natural with spiritual, and of all with the Lord, our admiration ceases entirely, or is altogether changed as to its quality. The work of redemption was the miracle of miracles. It was that by which the heavens and hells were reduced to order. It was that by which the proper mediums between the Lord and nature were restored, in consequence of which He may approach every man, whatever be his state, in a way consistent with his freedom and the divine order. It was that by which divine truth becomes veiled and accommodated to every possible condition of the human mind. Though in consequence of the existing disorders in the spiritual world, the effects produced were sometimes, to appearance, necessarily violent, yet is it the end and consummation of the work, to prevent the possibility of such effects, by removing their causes. Satan had, as it were, ascended up into heaven, and must therefore fall as lightning from heaven. But he has not only fallen, but is held in perpetual subjection. This work was not complete till the last judgment, and the formation of a new heaven and a new church, by which the way is opened for the restoration of perfect order and peace. "And I heard a great voice out of heaven, saying, behold the tabernacle of God is with men, and He will dwell with them, and they shall be his people, and God Himself shall be with them, their God."

The New Jerusalem Church has been ushered in by no miracles;* yet is the divine providence most clearly visible in the preparation for its descent, particularly in the general diffusion of knowledge in relation to the natural sciences. The discovery of the laws of the operations of nature may be regarded as the promise and the foretaste of the knowledge of the laws of the spiritual world also. The mystery which overhung the occult sciences has vanished. Their power to hold the multitude in awe no longer exists. They are no longer the secret of a privileged set of men, but are opened to the scrutiny of every eye. It is not, perhaps, a matter of surprise that as the clouds, which superstition and imposture had superinduced, were dispersed, a total disbelief of the connection of the sciences with spiritual things should be the first effect; that a feeling of the presence of the angel of the Lord should not instantly succeed the

* There are well attested facts recorded of Swedenborg, which, if credited by those out of the New Church, must appear to them miraculous. But these facts are not appealed to as evidence of the doctrines of this Church; on the other hand, they are so explained and elucidated by the new truths which are revealed, as to be mostly, if not wholly, deprived of their miraculous aspect.

fears of imaginary spectres. But were man to continue to look no farther than to this world for the causes of natural phenomena, it would have been better for him to have continued to regard the thunderings and lightnings, the revolution of the sun, moon and stars, and innumerable other phenomena, as the effect of the immediate presence of Jehovah. It was not well that he should lay aside his admiration and fear, to gaze on these operations in a state of senseless apathy; but it was well that after he had heard the voice from Him who walks on the troubled sea, "be not afraid," that he should be thereby prepared for a still further manifestation of the divine power and presence, in that he says, "I am." The arm of the Lord has been withdrawn from human view only that the world may be prepared to see and acknowledge its connection with his body. The overwhelming sense of the divine omnipotence has been removed, that man might thereby be permitted to approach the divine love and wisdom. A state of liberty is now enjoyed which has not before existed in the world, and the salvation or the condemnation will be great in proportion.

CONSCIENCE.

PREVIOUS to the time of Locke, the opinion generally prevailed that mankind possessed certain innate ideas, or ideas at the time of their birth. This opinion was opposed by that metaphysician; and the opposite views have been since gaining ground, and are now hardly questioned. Locke, however, appears to have been entirely ignorant of the real condition and character of the infant mind. He always thought of it as something to be filled up with materials from without. The fact of its development and of the adaptation of the external world to this end, seems never to have occurred to him. Had this occurred to him, he might have seen that ideas were the natural and necessary effect of this development, and that the infant may be said to possess them about as much, and in the same way, as he may be said to have teeth. Neither the one nor the other would be consistent with his present state of reception and dependence; but both exist in effort, and will certainly appear in their appointed seasons.

The fault of Locke was, that he did not see that the originating cause of ideas was in the soul itself, or rather above the soul, in the Lord. He saw only the back door, and even that opened the wrong way. He considered the two sources of ideas to be sensation and reflection. That is, he supposed that they were first received through the senses, and afterwards new ideas were formed by reflection. Thus he made sensation virtually their only source, and this doctrine has been since avowed by his followers. It is true that the senses are necessary to the formation of ideas, but not in the way that Locke supposed. They are necessary to the formation of ideas, because it is there that the affections of the mind leaf and blossom. The spiritual part of man is not a vacuum to receive painted images, but a substance, in the constant effort of passing forth out of itself into the external world. The seed which is planted is the cause of the tree, although the earth may furnish the substances which are necessary to its growth—in like manner is the soul the cause of ideas, and it meets the external world in the outer court of the senses, not to be brought down to a level with it, but to make it tributary to its own form and determination.

The opinion that conscience is innate, prevails extensively with those who have abandoned that of innate ideas. It is often spoken of as a monitor, and is supposed to give the same admonition to all, whatever may be their state. It is considered as, in itself, a revelation prior in time to the Sacred Scripture, and not less absolute in kind. This view in regard to conscience is altogether fallacious. It possesses nothing of this fixed and universal character; but is infinitely various according to the moral and intellectual condition of individuals. Indeed it has sometimes appeared to me that consciousness, used in its broadest sense as applied to the will as well as the understanding, was a more appropriate and expressive word than conscience. So far as man is regenerated, in addition to the consciousness of the good and the true in the will and the understanding, exists the consciousness that these are derived from the Lord, the only source of goodness and truth; and this is conscience with the spiritual, and perception with the celestial man. But the consciousness of the merely natural man does not commence at the source of his existence, but with himself; and this is not conscience or true consciousness. The possessions of his mind, not proceeding from the source of life, do not partake of its sustaining conservative power, but are perishable. His consciousness possesses the quality of that of which he is conscious, and is not living, but dead.

That conscience is not of a universal, absolute kind, may be obvious to any one from the state of uncivilized savage nations. Their crimes appear to be in all respects natural to them; and they exhibit no indications of being sensible that they are crimes. Our Lord says of the Jews, "If I had not come and spoken unto them, they had not had sin; but now they have no cloak for their sin." Had not our Lord come into the world, the power of distinguishing between good and evil, the true and the false, would have been utterly lost; and mankind would have been rendered free from actual sin, by the accumulated weight of hereditary evil. Even when he did come, "He was in the world and the world was made by Him, and the world knew Him not." As the power of distinguishing between good and evil would have been lost, had not the Lord come into the world, so is its continuance solely the effect of the influence of the Word. "That was the true light, that lighteth every man that cometh into the world." That conscience is not universal may also be obvious from the fact, that what offends the conscience of one has no effect on that of another. If it were absolute, it should be universally the same; but this is evidently not the case.

In the last state of a church many forms and words remain, after they have ceased to be filled with their true spirit and meaning. When our Lord was upon earth, the Jews were apparently conscientious in all their acts in relation to him. The letter of their law seemed to them to be violated by the very spirit by which it was fulfilled; so opposite was this spirit to that by which they were governed. They could not bear to see the sick healed on the sabbath day; for they were unwilling to acknowledge the Son of Man Lord also of the sabbath. They said, behold a gluttonous man and a wine bibber, a friend to publicans and sinners. The Lord appeared to them to violate the letter of the Word in fulfilling it, because to do the commandments in freedom, from love, was something of which they had never formed a conception. Hence during the glorification of the human, in proportion as external restraints were removed and the Father became manifest in his works, the Lord seemed to them to do violence to their conscience, till he was at last crucified as a blasphemer. What true conscience is, had become again unknown in the world till it was revealed in the spiritual sense of the Word. Mankind had become wedded to external forms, and to self-derived doctrines springing from faith alone. They had fallen into the errors which were rebuked by our Lord while upon earth, when they disfigured their faces, and for a pretence made long prayers; forgetful that our heavenly Father knows what things we have need of before we ask Him. They sometimes seem to have mistaken the spleen for the heart, and the morbid sensation induced by disease for the pains of a tender conscience. If true conscience co-exist with the faith of three persons in the Godhead or a denial of the Lord's divinity, it is because these doctrines are not inwardly believed; for true conscience involves the consciousness that He is the vine and we are the branches.

The belief that the misery of the wicked in the future state results from the remorse of conscience, is entirely groundless. All who possess true conscience are in the heavens. It is known that the conscience becomes hardened or "seared" by continued habits of evil; and, consequently, that the worse a man is, the less of conscience he has. If, therefore, the misery of the hells were from this source, the sufferings of the wicked would be inversely as their evils; for the conscience ceases to be susceptible of pain, as it ceases to be living. True conscience is given only so far as the work of regeneration is accomplished; but there is a semblance of conscience which arises from the remains of infancy and childhood. During this period all men are susceptible of good influences—their angels do always behold the face of their Father who is in heaven. As the child advances in life, the impressions produced by these states are not lost, but stored up as a heavenly treasure. As in later periods his hereditary evils acquire strength and activity, there is a perception of incongruity or opposition between these evils and those early impressions. Hence the latter operate as a restraint on the former. There is thus a warning voice which descends from the depths of the soul; but it is only an indistinct murmur, without any articulate words. If this voice is not heeded it will become less and less audible, till it is no longer heard in the distance. But if this voice is regarded—if it lead him to shun evils as sins, and direct him to the Sacred Scripture for life and light, what was a confused sound will gradually become articulate speech; and he "will hear a word behind him, saying, This is the way, walk thou in it, when he turns to the right hand, and when he turns to the left."

HOME.

The following extract is from the Introduction to Entomology, by Kirby and Spence. It probably accords with facts within the knowledge of most readers.

"When bees have found the direction in which their hive lies, Huber says they fly to it with an extreme rapidity, and as straight as a ball from a musket: and if their hives were always in open situations, one might suppose, as Huber seems inclined to think, that it is by their sight they are conducted to them. But hives are frequently found in small gardens embowered in wood, and in the midst of villages surrounded and interspersed with trees and buildings, so as to make it impossible that they can be seen from a distance. If you had been with me in 1815, in the famous Pays de Waes in Flanders—where the country is a perfect flat, and the inhabitants so enamored either of the beauty or profit of trees, that their fields, which are rarely above three acres in extent, are *constantly* surrounded with a double row, making the whole district one vast wood—you would have pitied the poor bees, if reduced to depend on their own eye-sight for retracing the road homeward. In vain, during my stay at St. Nicholas, I sallied out at every outlet to try to gain some idea of the extent and form of the town. Trees—trees—trees—still met me, and intercepted the view in every direction; and I defy any inhabitant bee of this rural metropolis, after once quitting its hive, ever to gain a glimpse of it again until nearly perpendicularly over it. The bees, therefore, of the Pays de Waes, and consequently all other bees, must be led to their abodes by instinct, as certainly as it is instinct that directs the migrations of birds or of fishes, or domestic quadrupeds, to find out their homes from inconceivable distances."

The love of home, in some form or other, is universally felt and acknowledged. It is the foundation of patriotism, and is often made the theme of poetry. The first idea of home is that of the place of nativity. The early affections are particularly connected with the place and scenes in which they were developed; and as they are excited, if this connection has been severed, there is often a sensation of pain, yet of such a kind, that it may perhaps be called pleasurable, and rarely fails to be cherished. Whatever awakens to the greatest degree the pleasurable feelings which we cherished in any particular place, will bring the strongest attachment to that place. The influence of music in this respect is universally known, and the story of desertions produced among the Swiss troops from hearing their national air, is not probably new to my readers. In animals the affection and the understanding being inseparable, the love of home involves the knowledge of where it is. But as man became what he is pleased to call rational, he lost his instinct—as he undertook to guide and direct himself, he refused the spontaneous guidance of the Lord, which is freely given and was once freely received. His way is interspersed with guide-boards, to inform him of the direction of his journey and the distance he has to pass. He has eaten of the tree of knowledge of good and evil, and become as God. It is true that he has learned to read and write, but it is also true that he has lost that intuitive perception, which it is the sole object of letters, under the Divine Providence, ultimately to restore. There is, however, a part of the soul where it is not even in the power of man wholly to pervert its influence. His reason may wonder at the involuntary operations which are going on in his own body, but cannot control them; and although, ever since he left the garden of Eden, he has been as it were homeless, yet there is a region within him where instinct has always remained, and into instinct it will be the perfection of learning and science to return. It ought not, however, to be forgotten, that human instinct must always differ from that of brutes, as much as man differs from animals.

In the spiritual world every man goes instinctively to his own place, for his state makes his place, and his relation to those with whom he is associated cannot but be felt and acknowledged. There is something analogous to this in this world also, for here every man has some ruling love, some peculiar determination of mind, which exerts a central power on all his subordinate thoughts and affections. However his mind may wander, this is not forgotten; for this is the very seat and source of memory. Those who are of the New Church have occasion to be surprised at the changes they experience. It is necessary for their instruction and regeneration that they should pass from one society of spirits to another. Were it not for this ruling love—this instinct of home, they would wander like a mariner without a compass, without object or even distinct consciousness. But this instinct exerts a controlling power over all their changes, and converts them to use. However far they may have travelled, there is one place which they have not left, and cannot leave, except by degrees, and as another is provided. This is home, the common centre and measure of all the changes they experience. Were it not for the influence that this instinct exerts, insanity would inevitably ensue; and it is worthy of consideration whether insanity is not frequently occasioned by a partial destruction of this instinct, from habits of mental or bodily dissipation. The consciousness must become indistinct, and all the possessions of the mind indeterminate; and the individual is for the most part disposed to wander in reality, as he does spiritually, with no proper end in view. But with those who shun evils as sins, and look to the Lord, the vein of use within them is constantly becoming more and more apparent; all their affections and thoughts more determinate; their consciousness more living and distinct, and they feel that they are approaching the place which the Lord has prepared for them.

SELF-LOVE.

We every where find, in the spiritual sense of the Word, that self-love is absolutely and essentially evil.* The evil is not in the degree in which it is exercised, nor in its being exercised blindly and without prudence; but is one and the same thing with the affection itself. Perhaps there is no subject on which the natural man is more blind than this. Full of love as it is, it even seems to him to be a hard doctrine. It seems to be unnatural that the circle of his affections, be-

* The love of self is good when there exists within it the love of others, or when self is loved for the sake of others. It is thus our duty to take proper care of ourselves, in order that we may be able to perform well our uses in life. But the love of self is evil when others are loved only for the sake of self. In the one case, we have regard to ourselves that we may be useful to others, in the other case we regard others only so far as they can be made serviceable to ourselves.

ginning with himself and extending to his relatives and friends, should be disturbed; and natural affection he regards as an essential virtue. He considers those who regard self-love as an evil, and are endeavoring to subdue it by shunning evils as sins, as attempting an impossibility. Perhaps he doubts their sincerity; and finds much in external appearances to confirm him in the belief that they are really governed by the same motives with himself. Their actions, he says, all tend to their own advantage. They are engaged in employments of honor or profit; and the honor or profit seems to him to be that by which they are stimulated to act. If he find any whose actions are apparently disinterested, he thinks it is either because they find the same kind of pleasure in that course, that he does in his, or have made a cold calculation of the future profit, and govern themselves accordingly. In either case it seems to him to be self-love in a different form. In these last days of the church, these views are justified by men who consider themselves, and are regarded by others, as religious, and are even attempted to be established as principles of religion. To the natural man they are exceedingly plausible, for they spring from his own feelings, and perfectly accord with them. Natural reason comes in to prove that these feelings are right. It is said to be wrong to contend with the nature which God has given us; and respect for self and for the dignity of human nature is inculcated as a duty. Self-love is blasphemously ascribed to the Lord himself; and a regard to his own glory is considered as the cause of the creation and preservation of the universe. The truth that self-love is in itself essentially evil is peculiar to the New Church.

The world knows still less in regard to what is good, than in regard to what is true. The distinction between truth and falsehood has never been entirely lost. Mankind have been, and naturally are, insensible to the spirit of truth. They have not acknowledged its true source; and have been incapable of seeing any truths except those of the most external kind. But that certain propositions are true, and that those which are directly opposed to them are false, all men in this world are compelled to admit. But the distinction between good and evil, love and self-love, is less apparent; and *the opposition* between them still more difficult to be discerned and acknowledged. What the natural man considers good, passes by such gentle gradations into what is obviously forbidden, that no line of demarcation exists. For example, what he regards as his first duty, self-preservation, is, in the accomplishment of its ends, so interwoven with the desire to obtain the property of others, that they are obviously parts of the same whole. His self-respect can exist only by a tacit comparison of himself with his neighbor, in which is latently involved contempt or hatred of the latter. Conjugial love is to him simply the love of the sex circumscribed, in all its original unchastity. All his affections are apparently human, but in their tendencies and affinities, they are completely bestial. They are like the faces and bodies of men, with the extremities of serpents.

Not only is some sort of distinction and opposition between truth and falsehood seen and acknowledged; but reason is compelled to acknowledge also that it cannot of itself make a thing true or false. Thus the laws of the natural sciences are known to be absolute and unconditional in their existence; and all that man can do is to discover them. In this way, truth is seen to be something independent of the mind itself, not its own creation; and may be in some faint degree referred to the Lord as the Creator. But with goodness it is otherwise. The feelings obviously have an internal, not an external origin; and as the natural man, when he turns inward, does not look beyond himself, they seem to be wholly self-originated. The dispositions of individuals are subjects of praise or dispraise, without a thought that the good is from the Lord or the evil from the hells. Thus good and evil being ascribed to the same source, are necessarily confounded. True goodness is not known. Different names are only applied to self-love, as it is differently manifested—as we might apply one name to the affection by which the wild beast is stimulated to tear in pieces her prey, and another to that by which she is led to give it fondly to her offspring.

Thus has the natural man become as God,

knowing good and evil. In the ascription of goodness to himself is latently involved the belief that he is himself divine; for "there is none good but one, God." This belief may not assume a distinct form in this world. It receives a check in the understanding. The facts which have been acquired from the Sacred Scripture relative to the existence and character of God, remain in the external memory, and modify the persuasions which arise from evil. Many things also force upon him the confession of his own weakness; particularly the knowledge of his own mortality. The remains of infancy and childhood also, are not yet entirely extinguished; and the voice which is sometimes heard from them, as the faint cries of a child in distress, produces a momentary perception of the reality of heavenly things. It is only occasionally in this world, when the understanding has, from some cause, lost its power to correct or to conceal the state of the will, that men openly believe and declare that they are gods. Such are regarded and treated as insane. The source of the disorder, as existing in the evil of the will, is entirely overlooked; and the understanding which does not prevent the manifestation of that persuasion, which exists in the natural mind of every man in whom the evil has not been subdued by being shunned as a sin, is charged with the insanity. But in the other world the true character is more fully developed. Self-love, as it has no bounds to its desires, so has it no bounds to its false persuasions. The knowledges in regard to the Lord which have been acquired from the Scriptures are cast aside by those who are confirmed in evil, for they are not the garments with which their affections can clothe themselves. The sense of weakness induced by the fear of natural death, is removed. The vague persuasion that if there was a God, he would be seen by them, if they continued to live after death, has not been realized. All fear, if any exist, is speedily removed, and freedom of thought and action restored by the presence of those spirits with whom they were associated without their knowledge, when in the natural world. Their self-love, if it continue to be that by which they are governed, as they sink into hell, openly asserts its own supremacy, and is kept in check only by the contending claims of their miserable associates.

The quality of self-love cannot be discerned without first understanding what love is. And here it must be remarked that although the word is, and has been in the mouths of all men, the disclosure of its source and true quality is one of the distinguishing characteristics of the New Church. There is, ordinarily, in the minds of men, the moment they ascend above material things, a total want of reality. .As the soul itself is not regarded as an organized substance, so neither does it seem to require to be acted upon by aught that is substantial. But there is a sun in the spiritual world, as there is in the natural; and as from the latter there is an emanation of heat and light, which is essential to animal and vegetable life, so from the former there is an emanation of spiritual heat and light, the first of which is of love, and the last of wisdom. The sober realities of the New Church are sometimes the poetry of the Old. That which seems real to the latter, only on the condition of their transferring to it somewhat of themselves, interweaving it with their own imaginations, giving it the indirect support of their own arm, and tracing its connection with their own earth; with the former is not only real, but the source of all realities. That the Lord should be asked in prayer to warm the heart and enlighten the understanding, or, when represented in a picture, that his head should be radiant with light, is considered as in good taste; but the simple truth that his face actually shines as the sun, and that he is really the source of heat and light to all the angels in the heavens, is startling and visionary. Had it been possible for him, as he ascended up into heaven, to have been visible to those in opposite states of mind, the one would have been lost in wonder at the apparently miraculous suspension of the law of gravitation; the other, in adoration of Him from whose constant energy all worlds are held in their places.

The Lord causes the sun of the spiritual world to rise on the evil and the good. But with the former it is turned into darkness, and they do not even know that it exists. To such its influence would even seem to be the source of darkness, because it would be inconsistent with all which they call light. Owls and bats are created through those who thus turn day into night and night into day, and exactly correspond to and represent their state. But with the good the Lord is a sun and a shield, and there shall be no night with them. There is an objection to the use of the most common words in our language, because they are coupled with ideas altogether inadequate to what they ought to convey. Love and Wisdom are regarded out of the New Church as purely abstract terms,—and when it is said that the Lord created the world from Love by Wisdom, nothing more would be understood, than that he was prompted to the work by feelings of benevolence, and the work was wisely planned. But it is now revealed that the work of creation commences in the souls of angels and men, and that the spiritual heat and light which there impart warmth and intelligence, as they pass outward, actually create and sustain all things in the natural world.

Something may be seen in regard to what love is,

from the nature and effects of that which corresponds to it—the heat of the natural sun. In the winter, all vegetable and a considerable proportion of animal life is suspended. But in the spring, the fields are clothed with verdure; the trees put forth their leaves and blossoms; those animals which have been in a state of torpor, revive; the birds choose their mates, build their nests, and fill the air with their music, and all things are filled with the effort of reproduction and preservation which is pressing into them from the Lord the Creator. The heat of spring as it descends on the vegetable world, does not change the quality of any thing—it does not destroy the bad and preserve the good; but causes all to grow and bring forth fruit. But some bring forth fruit which is delightful to the taste and useful for the sustenance of man, and others that which is poisonous, or merely thorns and thistles. So also does this heat call forth the latent energies of all animals, without changing the quality of any. Those which are torpid, it revives; and to those which are alive, it gives more life. So it is with spiritual heat and light, as they fall on the heavens and the hells. They cause both the one and the other to bring forth fruit; but the fruit of the one is good, and that of the other is evil. Those who are branches of the true vine, perceive and acknowledge the source of their life; and this life is the simple undivided effort to bring forth good fruit. But the evil are apparently men, and seem to themselves and to others to bear fruit. But this fruit, in consequence not only of the absence of all desire to be useful to others, but from the inward endeavor to do them injury, becomes in some cases like that of a poisonous tree; and in others, results in the abortive and sterile effort of the thorn and the thistle. It should be remarked, however, that whereas the nature of beasts and vegetables is fixed, and the heat simply causes the manifestation of their peculiar life; the quality of men in this world is not thus fixed, and it is the constant effort of the Divine Love and Wisdom to subdue our evil affections. "No man can come unto me except the Father who hath sent me draw him." It is the endeavor of the Divine Love and Wisdom to pass forth into and through man unchanged in their quality; and this endeavor is effectual so far as is consistent with his free-agency. We ought also to be careful while we direct the mind to natural heat and light, in order to avoid the error that Divine Love and Wisdom are unsubstantial, lest we think of the Spiritual Sun in any degree unconnected with the Lord, and forget that all spiritual heat and light are of the Word in whom was life; and the life was the light of men.

It is the simple undivided effort of spiritual heat and light to cause men to bring forth good fruit, without taking any thought for themselves. "Herein is my Father glorified, that ye bear much fruit; so shall ye be my disciples." "Therefore take no thought, saying, what shall we eat? or what shall we drink? or wherewithal shall we be clothed? For after all these things do the gentiles seek; for your heavenly Father knoweth that ye have need of all these things. But seek ye first the kingdom of God and his righteousness, and all these things shall be added unto you." "This is my commandment, that ye love one another, as I have loved you." "Whosoever exalteth himself shall be abased; and he that humbleth himself, shall be exalted." These are not arbitrary commandments, to be rewarded in an arbitrary way; they are the essential laws of true humanity. It is an inverted effort for a man to think of himself. The creative endeavor is always that of development; that by which the internal passes outward into the external—good affections into corresponding acts of usefulness. The eye cannot see itself. It is not easy for an individual to conceive distinctly and correctly the peculiar expression of his own countenance, and the effort is not unattended with pain; and this for the plain reason, that by the attempt the powers of the mind are diverted from their proper channel, and the current of life turned back upon itself. No organ in the human body regards itself in its use. All these organs have distinct and separate offices to perform; but it is not for itself that the heart sends forth the blood; it is not for themselves that the veins return it. It is not for itself that the liver secretes the bile; it is not for themselves that the absorbents select the chyle from the digested food; or that the glands detect any poison which may be lurking in the system. The latter represent a purely disinterested affection, in themselves suffering disease, in the effort to protect the other parts. There is no image of self-love in the uses of any of the organs of the human body; for these organs perform their functions from that life which is above the control of ourselves. The first traces of selfishness are discovered not in the healthy activity of the parts, but in their diseases; and that organ which refuses to perform its duty to the rest is the first occasion and seat of the disease. As all the organs of the body are instruments of usefulness, so is the human form which they go to compose, a perfect image, and when governed by life from the Lord, a perfect endeavor of use to the neighbor. The forms of external politeness—the expressions of friendship, and of dispositions of usefulness to those with whom they have transactions, which even the worst men are obliged hypocritically to assume, convey but an imperfect idea of what we were designed to be in reality.

Thus it is that those who act from that life which

is constantly flowing into them from the Lord, without perverting it, fill their own uses from the simple love of those uses. In doing this, they are indeed happy; and they are not permitted to be destitute of any means of use which would be made subservient to a true love of duty. But when does this love from the Lord, which is thus essentially expansive and communicative, become self-love? How totally is its quality changed, when, instead of passing forth in gladness into its own works, it becomes confined and self-directed? What would have been a creating and invigorating heat, now becomes a burning and consuming fire. There cannot be a more perfect contradiction in words than is involved in the expression, self-love. It means love deprived of every distinguishing property by which it is constituted —love destroyed—death. This is that of which the Lord speaks when he says, "Then shall he say also unto them on the left hand, Depart from me, ye cursed, into everlasting fire, prepared for the devil and his angels: for I was an hungered and ye gave me no meat; I was thirsty and ye gave me no drink; I was a stranger and ye took me not in; naked and ye clothed me not; sick and in prison and ye visited me not."

The revelation which the Lord is making to his New Church, is not only a revelation of Truth, but of Goodness. "But the time cometh when I shall no longer speak to you in proverbs; but I shall shew you plainly of the Father." Heaven itself, with its delights, is now freely offered to all who wish to receive it. The Lord has come a second time, and a second time is he rejected. There has been another earthquake, and the veil of the temple no longer conceals the holy of holies. The New Jerusalem is about to realize all that the Christian church, in its best estate, vaguely anticipated. The latter, at farthest, did but see the grapes, the pomegranates, and the figs, brought by the spies from the land of Canaan; the former is permitted to partake freely of the milk and honey with which it overflows. That goodness is now revealed by which the heavens are created and sustained; and in its revelation it displays the quality and opposition of that evil by which the hells are influenced.

EXTERNAL RESTRAINT.

"The prevalence of the plague," says the Baltimore Gazette, "has always been marked by licentiousness and depravity. Thucidides thus speaks of the manners of the people during the plague at Athens. 'For people now dared to do many things openly which they were heretofore compelled by shame to conceal; and they calculated on their sudden change of fortune, seeing that many of the rich perished, while those who formerly were destitute became rich with their property. They therefore deemed it right to set about the immediate enjoyment of it, and gave up all their mind to pleasures, considering they might, in turn, be deprived of their treasures and life itself in a few days. Nor was any individual disposed to undertake any labor for an honorable reward, because he thought it uncertain whether he might not die before he could obtain it. Whatever each person deemed agreeable or lucrative to himself, he considered as expedient and honorable; and he did not allow himself to be restrained in the pursuit by the fear of God or human laws.'

"The plague at Marseilles was as fruitful in horrors. M. Bertrand says,—'While the arm of the Lord was yet extended over us, a general license was seen to reign among the people, and depravity of morals frightful to think on. Some seized on houses left vacant by the mortality; others forced open those which were shut up, or guarded by persons incapable of resistance. They entered those where, perhaps, there remained only one person languishing with the malady, forced open the drawers and closets, and took away whatever they found most precious, often carrying their guilt to the length of delivering themselves from an opportune witness who otherwise had but a few moments to live.' "

Few realize, to what the natural man is continually inclined, and what crimes would be perpetrated, were it not for external restraints. We are told by Swedenborg that the natural man is of himself continually inclined to the lowest hell, and that he is withdrawn and withheld solely by the Divine influence. Swedenborg also informs us, that man is of himself more savage than the wild beasts. This appears to be strong language. Yet it is not only true, but capable of demonstration; for in evil spirits and men is the very fountain of the life by which these beasts are impelled to action.

The natural man grows up under restraints imposed by the order of society and the civil law, of the extent of which he is himself ignorant. He is not aware that the life externally correct, is not internally good also, till he begins to shun evils, not because they are disreputable or dangerous, but because they are sins. The true quality of his own life is then revealed to him, as he is able to see it. He is generally impressed with the belief that he is worse than any one else; for he dares not impute to others such tendencies as he finds in himself. Such a persuasion, however, is not true, nor does it possess all the humility which it appears to have. It is not unattended with the latent belief, that as his evil is his own, so he still has of himself, (perhaps to a very small degree,) something good. But true humility perceives that one man is of himself neither better nor worse than his neighbor; for all are of themselves essentially evil. There is none good but one, God; nor can any thing good exist for a moment, independent of its source.

If the man who leads a moral life, but is as yet

insensible of his own evil tendencies, would know what he is internally, let him reflect how he would appear to those around him, if every affection and thought of which he is conscious, were made visible to those in whose company he is. In the present state of society, the power of concealment is common to all, and is by all insensibly practised. But if any one in his natural state should from any cause lose the power of suppressing the spontaneous suggestions of his heart, he would at once be excluded from all society, though this society may differ from him in no other respect, than that of possessing the power which he has lost.

Herein exists a remarkable difference between the spiritual world and the natural. In the former, things without represent the true quality of things within, being created directly from them, and bearing their image. The affections and thoughts pass forth and become actually visible in the things which correspond to them. But in the natural world, the spontaneous thoughts for the most part are not permitted to pass forth, till they have been scrutinized and are thought to answer. It is to a considerable extent the case, that the opposite is instantly and almost imperceptibly substituted for the true thought. This is often an important ingredient in the politeness of artificial society.

It might perhaps at first thought have been supposed, that such a scourge as the plague would have made men more honest in their dealings, and more inclined to seriousness and religion. But we learn from history that the opposite is the fact. Cold calculations and distant prospects of gratification, which had served as safety-valves, are suddenly checked; and the dominant passions seize on their objects, with an impetuosity which displays their true character. The usual influence of the fear of death is removed, when there seems to be no chance for escape; and men begin to act as they would if they were already in the spiritual world.

HEREDITARY EVIL.

There are two prevailing opinions in the world, in regard to hereditary evil both of which are equally at variance with the truth. By some, man is supposed, in consequence of Adam's transgression, to be by nature entirely destitute of holiness, and altogether sinful; and by others, he is thought to come into the world perfectly pure and free from all evil. Both agree in regarding his state, whether considered good or evil, as in a certain sense miraculous. By the one, his condition is thought to have some miraculous connection with the first transgression, and to require for his regeneration a miraculous interference of the Holy Spirit; by the other, the soul is supposed at the commencement of its existence to come in a miraculous manner from God, and to be pure, and of course to need no regeneration. False views in regard to the origin and nature of the soul are so universal at the present day, as to meet us every where and on every subject.

We learn from the doctrines of the New Church, that the spirit of man is substantial; and that this, as well as the material body, is derived from our natural parents; the internal from the father, and the external from the mother. The quality and peculiar character of the offspring of course depend on the quality of those from whom it is derived. This is the ground of the peculiarities observable in nations and families. The external marks of resemblance among those of the same nation, tribe, and family, are subjects of universal observation. To the New Church it is known that the features of the body correspond to and represent the character of the mind. It is not true that man is born a sinner; for sin implies the actual appropriation and commission of evil. But it is true that he is born filled with hereditary evils; with dispositions to external sins of every kind. Spiritual diseases as well as natural are hereditary; for the latter are only the correspondences and effects of the former. But it is also true, that for every disease there is provided a remedy; and that no one is condemned for his hereditary evils, unless he adopts them into his life, and by acting from them makes them his own. All who die in infancy and childhood, are instructed by the angels, and gradually withdrawn from their evils, and thus introduced into heaven. So would it be with all

14*

who continue to years of maturity in this world, if they lived according to the light which is given them.

But there are many in the world at the present day, who deny the existence of hereditary evil altogether, and of course the necessity of regeneration. Such persons know comparatively nothing either in regard to what they are, or what they were designed to be. Their external conduct may appear fair, and they may be kind to their relatives and friends; but there are depths in their hearts of which they have no knowledge. It is in the order of Divine Providence that our evils should be revealed to us, just as fast as we are prepared to see and shun them as sins; and thus become recipients of the opposite goods. But those who are in no degree prepared to make this acknowledgment, do not see them as evils. They seem to live of and from themselves, and their life appears to them to be altogether a good thing. Their evils never having been developed, are not known to exist. These evils resemble the young of wild beasts, which in their sleep or playfulness seem docile and innocent. The following extract may illustrate the real character of some affections, which, previous to their development, seem as harmless and innocent as the young tiger.

"A party of gentlemen from Bombay, one day visiting the stupendous cavern-temple of Elephanta, discovered a tiger's whelp in one of the obscure recesses of the edifice. Desirous of kidnapping the cub, without encountering the fury of its dam, they took it up hastily and cautiously, and retreated. Being left entirely at liberty, and extremely well fed, the tiger grew rapidly, appeared tame, and fondling as a dog, and in every respect domesticated. At length, when having attained a vast size, and, notwithstanding its apparent gentleness, it began to inspire terror by its tremendous powers of doing mischief, a piece of raw meat, dripping with blood, fell in its way. It is to be observed, that up to that moment it had been studiously kept from raw animal food. The instant, however, it had dipped its tongue in blood, something like madness seemed to have seized the animal—a destructive principle, hitherto dormant, was awakened—it darted fiercely, and with glaring eyes, upon its prey, tore it with fury to pieces, and, growling and roaring in the most fearful manner, rushed off towards the jungles."—*Brown's Anecdotes.*

MARRIAGE IN THE HEAVENS.

[It is evident that no considerable progress can be made in understanding the human mind, or the laws of its development, without a knowledge of the essential distinction between the sexes. This subject, from its nature being particularly exposed to profanation, has hitherto been providentially withheld from view. It has, so to speak, been provided with a lock for its special protection. The passage of Scripture where it is said that "in the resurrection they neither marry nor are given in marriage," seems to have had the effect, on many minds, to silence inquiry, and has usually been considered unanswerable, when suggestions have been raised on the subject of the future, or, what is the same thing, the spiritual distinction between the sexes. But the time has come when further light may be safely given; and He who has the key has opened from within, what men would have attempted in vain to have opened from without. There are some to whom it is thought that the following suggestions may be useful; with others they will have no weight.]

The belief has prevailed in the Christian Church, and is perhaps nearly universal, that in the future state of existence there is no distinction of sex, and no relation of husband and wife. This belief exactly accords with the vague notions that exist of spirits and spiritual things. An idea of the spiritual is attempted to be formed by taking away all the properties of matter; and one of the first steps is to deny to spirits a form. Thus the spiritual becomes one with the incomprehensible.

Its being said that "in the resurrection they neither marry nor are given in marriage," is thought to be evidence of the truth of such opinions as have been mentioned. But such is not the fact. It would be difficult to name a falsity which might not apparently, or indeed which has not in reality, been confirmed from the letter of the Word. This is of Divine permission. The falsities themselves always spring from an evil heart of unbelief;—and those parts of the Sacred Scripture which seem to be the occasion of them, are in reality only pressed into their service. As the Lord was born of a woman, inheriting from her the evils of the Jewish nation, so the truths of the Word, as they descended into the letter, were modified by the actual state of mankind with which they came in contact. These truths, purely divine in themselves, took their body from the state of the Jewish nation; and it is only by those who enter within the veil, and view the letter from the spirit, that this body is seen to be glorified, and this humanity to be Divine. The Divine Truth, that chaste conjugial love, proceeding from the union of goodness and truth in the Lord Himself, is the source of the happiness of the angels of heaven, as it falls on "an evil and adulterous generation," becomes gradually obscured and totally perverted. The following relation of Swedenborg is so full of instruction on the subject, that it is introduced entire.

"Having awaked from sleep at midnight, I saw, at some height towards the east, an angel holding in his right hand a paper, which, from influent light from the sun, appeared in resplendent whiteness, in the middle of which was a writing in golden letters, and I saw written, THE MARRIAGE OF GOOD AND TRUTH; from the writing there flashed a splendor, which went forth into a wide circle around the paper; this circle or encompassing appeared thence as the dawn appears in spring time. After this I saw the angel descending with the paper in his hand,

and as he descended, the paper appeared less and less lucid, and that writing which was THE MARRIAGE OF GOOD AND TRUTH, changed from a golden color into a silver, then into a copper, afterwards into an iron, and at length into iron-rust and brass-rust color; and at last the angel was seen to pass into a dark cloud, and, through the cloud, upon the earth; and there that paper, although it was still held in the angel's hand, was not seen. This was in the world of spirits, into which all men after death first come together; and then the angel spake to me, saying, Ask those who come hither, whether they see me, or any thing in my hand? There came a multitude, an assemblage from the east, an assemblage from the south, an assemblage from the west, and an assemblage from the north; and I asked those who were arriving from the east and the south, who were those that in the world had given themselves to learning, whether they saw any one here with me, and any thing in his hand. They all said that they saw nothing at all. I then asked those who arrived from the west and the north, who were those that in the world had believed in the words of the learned; these said that they did not see any thing; but yet the last of these, who in the world had been in simple faith from charity, or in some truth from good, after the former had gone away, said, that they saw a man with a paper, a man in a becoming dress, and a paper upon which letters were traced; and when they brought their eyes nearer to it, they said, that they read, *The marriage of good and truth;* and these addressed the angel, begging him to tell what this was; and he said, that all things which are in the universal heaven, and all things which are in the universal world, are nothing else but a marriage of good and truth, since each and every thing, as well those which live and communicate life, as those which do not live and do not communicate life, was created from the marriage of good and truth; and into it there is not given any thing created into truth alone, nor any thing into good alone; the former or the latter solitary is not any thing, but by marriage they exist and become something of the same quality as the marriage is. In the Lord the Creator is divine good and divine truth in its own very substance, (the *esse* of his substance is divine good, and the *existere* of his substance is divine truth,) and is also in its own very union, for in him they infinitely make one; since those two in the Creator Himself are one, therefore also they are one in each and every thing created from Him; hereby also the Creator is conjoined with all things created from Himself in an eternal covenant as of marriage. The angel further said, that the Sacred Scripture, which proceeded immediately from the Lord, is in general and in particular a marriage of good and of truth; and because the church, which is formed by means of truth of doctrine and religion, which is formed by means of good of life according to truth of doctrine, is with Christians solely from the Sacred Scripture, it may be evident that the church in general and in particular is the marriage of good and truth; (that it is so, may be seen in the APOCALYPSE REVEALED, n. 373, 483.) The same which was said above concerning the marriage of good and truth, was also said concerning THE MARRIAGE OF CHARITY AND FAITH, since good is of charity, and truth is of faith. Some of the forementioned, who did not see the angel and the writing, still standing by, and hearing these things, said with a half-full mouth, Yes, surely we apprehend those things: but then the angel said to them, Turn yourselves away a little from me and speak in like manner; and they turned themselves away, and said with a full mouth, *Not so.* After this the angel spake concerning the MARRIAGE OF GOOD AND TRUTH with consorts, saying, that if their minds were in that marriage, the husband being truth and the wife the good of this truth, both would be in the delights of the blessedness of innocence, and thence in the happiness in which the angels of heaven are; in which state the prolific power of the husband would be in a continual spring, and thence in the effort and ability to propagate its own truth, and the wife in the continual reception of it from love; the wisdom, which is from the Lord with the men, is sensible of nothing more

15

grateful than to propagate its own truths; and the love of wisdom, which is with the wives there, is sensible of nothing more pleasant than to receive those truths as if in the womb, and thus to conceive, be pregnant with, and bring them forth: spiritual prolifications with the angels of heaven are such; and if you are willing to believe it, natural prolifications are also from that origin. The angel, after a salutation of peace, raised himself from the earth, and being borne through the cloud, ascended into heaven, and then the paper shone as before, according to the degrees of ascent; and behold, the circle which before appeared as the dawn, then let itself down, and dispelled the cloud which brought darkness upon the earth, and it became sun-shine."

The above relation explains how it is that the same words in the Sacred Scripture are capable of having two entirely opposite senses according to the subject treated of. The words written on the paper were not a mere abstract proposition; the truth constantly existed and derived its splendor from the Lord himself. Such is the case with all the truths of the Sacred Scripture; but in their descent their glory appears to be tarnished; celestial love seems converted into the fire of infernal hatred; and celestial truth into its corresponding falsity. The fact that the words have these opposite meanings is therefore simply an expression of the order of the Divine Influx through the heavens into the world of spirits, and thence into the hells.

"In the resurrection they neither marry nor are given in marriage." These words, to the Jews to whom they were originally addressed, conveyed all the truth on the subject which they were able to receive. Their minds were totally unreceptive of the most distant conception of the chastity of the angels; and a negation of all the feelings and thoughts which they had ever experienced in regard to the union of the sexes, was the nearest approach to the condition of heaven of which they were capable. This passage of Scripture is, in this respect, parallel with many others. Thus, in the Jewish observance of the Sabbath, a total cessation of labor seemed to be required, because the Jews were not in a state to act except from evil; but when the Lord was on earth, it was revealed that the Son of Man is Lord also of the Sabbath—that it is lawful to do well on the Sabbath-day; and to the spiritual man it is apparent, that this is not only lawful but essential to a right observance of the Sabbath. It is also said, "If any man come to me, and hate not his father, and mother, and wife, and children, and brethren, and sisters, yea, and his own life also, he cannot be my disciple." This cannot be supposed to be literally required, because we are expressly commanded to honor father and mother. The truth is, that these loves in the natural man are so evil and selfish, that, in coming to the Lord, the change which is necessary seems to threaten and to require their complete extinction. In like manner it is said to be easier for a camel to pass through the eye of a needle, than for a rich man to enter into the kingdom of heaven. This expression, in the letter, very naturally called from the disciples the exclamation, who then can be saved? Now there is nothing necessarily evil in the possession of riches. On the contrary, the love of property for the sake of use is pure and heavenly. But so perverted and evil was this love with the Jews, that, being wholly incompatible with the state of heaven, its complete extermination seemed to be required before they could enter into that state.

Thus it was true to the Jews that in the resurrection they neither marry nor are given in marriage.

It has been said that the same words in the Sacred Scripture are in different parts used in totally opposite senses. Thus marriage in heaven would mean the union of goodness and truth; for it is solely by this union that marriage is there effected; but in the hells it means the union of the evil and the false, for it is only by this union that they there marry and are given in marriage. It seems to be the latter union which is spoken of in the passage of Scripture which has been made the subject of these observations. Hence it is not said that in the spiritual world "they neither marry nor are given in marriage," but "in the resurrection;" by which is meant a resurrection from death unto life, from self-love and the love of the world to the love of the Lord and the neighbor; and it is added that "they are as the angels of God in heaven." "Jesus said unto her, I am the resurrection and the life; he that believeth in Me, though he were dead, yet shall he live; and whosoever liveth and believeth in Me, shall never die."

That such is sometimes the meaning of marrying and being given in marriage, is obvious from the following passage, where such a state of the world is described that it became necessary that mankind should be destroyed by a flood, or, in the spiritual sense, that the church was vastated by falsities. "But as the days of Noe *were*, so shall also the coming of the Son of Man be. For as in the days that were before the flood they were eating and drinking, marrying and given in marriage, until the day that Noe entered into the ark, and knew not until the flood came, and took them all away; so shall also the coming of the Son of M an be." By eating and drinking are signified the appropriation of evils and falses; and by marrying and being given in marriage, their conjunction. Hence it is said that "John came neither eating nor drinking." By John is signified the literal sense of the Word; and the ceasing to do evil,—the abstinence from the appropriation of the evil and false which is there required, is a necessary state of preparation for the coming of the Son of Man, who "came eating and drinking"—that is, appropriating Divine Good and Truth. But as the

Jews said, "behold a man gluttonous, and a wine-bibber;" as the good and the true in Him appeared in their eyes to be evil and false, so, had the first effect of this goodness and truth, the union of the angels in the heavens, been revealed to them, it would have filled their minds with profanity and lasciviousness.

To the merely natural mind no two things seem more incongruous than the love of the sex and religion—for the merely natural mind is essentially unchaste. It is to this cause that we are to ascribe the celibacy required of the Catholic priesthood, and practised by certain societies in our own country, usually called Shakers. To purify this love, has been deemed impossible; hence, as a substitute, the vain endeavor to cover it up and destroy it. But to enter into the kingdom of heaven, the Lord requires a chaste development of all the principles of humanity, and permits an abandonment of none. Even the very hairs of our head are numbered, and nothing is suffered to be lost. This love is the strongest in the human breast, because it is the inmost; and if the understanding attempt to root it out, it will itself be paralyzed, precisely in proportion to the success of its endeavor. If the other members of the body combine against the head, their squalid appearance will sooner or later betray the source of their own vitality.

It has been said that the literal sense of the Word is written according to appearances—adapted to the states of those to whom it is addressed. This is particularly obvious from the letter of the Old Testament in relation to the sexes. Concubinage and polygamy appeared to the Jews to meet the Divine approbation. The reason is, that they were of such a quality that they could not be restrained from them, and the Lord leaves all in freedom. "He saith unto them, Moses, because of the hardness of your hearts, suffered you to put away your wives; but from the beginning it was not so." It is here revealed that what appeared to the Jews to be a Divine command, was only the permission of an evil which could not be restrained. "And I say unto you, whosoever shall put away his wife, except it be for fornication, and shall marry another, committeth adultery: and whoso marrieth her which is put away, doth commit adultery. His disciples say unto him, if the case of the man be so with his wife, it is not good to marry." We here see that state of feeling in the natural minds of the disciples, which required the Divine Truth to be clothed in the language in which it was, when it was said, that "in the resurrection they neither marry nor are given in marriage." This was an accommodation to the state of the Jews at that time, as the permissions of Moses were at a previous period. The existence of a future state of rewards and punishments was now just beginning to be revealed, because the world had at no previous period been prepared for it. But what constituted the happiness of the heavens or the misery of the hells, was not revealed; for the church was not in a state to receive it. The literal sense of the Word serves as a guard and protection both to the good and the evil—to the good from the evil, and to the evil "lest they break through unto the Lord to gaze, and many of them perish." In the passage which is the subject of these remarks, the arm of the Lord seems to be made bare and distinctly visible for this purpose. By it, every unchaste affection, as it raises its eyes upward, is smitten with blindness; and the heavens above become invisible. It is a perfect expression of the entire change of the quality of the affections and delights, which is necessary in order to enter into the presence of the Lord. The rejection of the unchaste thoughts and feelings of the natural man, which is here required, is the first step towards a revelation of the quality of that love which constitutes heaven. This revelation the Lord is now making to the "holy city, New Jerusalem, coming down from God out of heaven, prepared as a bride adorned for her husband." It is now revealed how it is that "He which made them at the beginning made them male and female"—that this law of creation, descending from above the heavens, and leaving its image on angels and men, passes through the animal and vegetable kingdoms to the earth's remotest bounds. "None shall want her mate." It is now revealed that chaste conjugial love is the source of the happiness of the angels; that they live together, husbands and wives; that the influx by which they are created is the same with that by which they are joined together. It is now revealed that neither the male nor the female could exist except in relation to the other; and that what is neither male nor female cannot be human. It is now revealed that the Lord stands to the church in the relation of the Husband to the wife; and that the influence by which husbands and wives are conjoined to Him, is the same with that by which they are united with each other. "Let us be glad and rejoice, and give honor to Him: for the marriage of the Lamb is come, and His wife hath made herself ready."

"In the resurrection they neither marry nor are given in marriage;" but what God hath joined together, that they put not asunder. They simply abstain from disjoining the Divine Goodness and Truth, by which their own union is effected, and constantly and eternally preserved. Of themselves, they feel that they can do nothing but evil. They make no protestations of future and abiding love. All this is of self, and proceeds from the persuasion that self loves. But in the heavens they perceive that the Lord is the only source of Love and Wisdom—that the heat and light from which they live, proceed constantly from Him. They swear not at all, but their communication is yea, yea; nay, nay—a simple assent to the teachings of their Divine Master—and all promises which regard futurity are lost in the prayer, "Give us, this day, our daily bread."

CHILDREN'S BOOKS.

[The following is extracted from a notice of "Lessons for Children of the New Church." The book itself will be found full of interest and instruction to children, and to all that is childlike any where.]

One of the most common faults with children's books is, that they are too abstract. The power of generalizing is among the last which is developed, and not only so, but is rarely possessed in any great degree of perfection. The mass of mankind do not distinctly comprehend abstract general principles. It is difficult for their minds to be elevated into the region of true rationality. As they come within the sphere of the particulars with which they are conversant, they are fastened to them by an attraction which they have not learned to withstand. I would not undervalue the power of generalization in the mature mind. It seems to be essential to all true rationality. So far as we have not general principles by which all particulars are tested, we seem to be left to the mercy of accident, and to be constantly liable to dash our feet against the stones. The particular cases on which we are called upon to judge, may be the product of our own individual states and affections; the general principles by which they should be tested may be regarded as the product of the states and affections of truly organized societies, or rather as the laws by which they are governed. That particular cases should be tested by general principles, results therefore from the laws of charity, which require that every individual should love and serve his neighbor, and teach him that the Church is that neighbor; and true rationality and true neighborly love must spring up, and grow, and be perfected together.

The power of generalization is thus perfected, as the thoughts of the individual are gradually *extended* into the society or societies of spirits with which he is connected.* But abstraction sometimes results in mere fantasy; and this may be supposed to be the case whenever the extension of thought does not proceed from truly organized angelic societies. Every society in the heavens is in the human form, because it is willing, as one, to perform the uses of a man; and whoever comes under the influence of such a society, will find no room for mere theories, but his whole energies will be determined to active usefulness. But when the extension of thought is into infernal societies instead of heavenly, they will only help to swell the amount of individual fantasy and insanity.

* It is usually understood that a person generalizes when he perceives the common properties of external objects, and thus classifies and arranges them. This is the outside of the thing. The inside of it appears to be, to think not as an individual, but as a social man. This is the true source of generalization.

Now the end for which this extension of thought is permitted is, that the individual may act as one with those from whom he thinks; and it would not be more absurd to require of the child the duties of the man, than to expect of him the power of fully understanding and appreciating abstract truths. Swedenborg says that "with those who are in the persuasions of truth, that is, who are in persuasive faith, the ideas of the thought are exceedingly confined." How much more true is this of the child, whose duty and prerogative is not reason, but submission and obedience?

The child is little and must therefore have a little book. So far is plain. But how often has the very next step been a fatally false one? How often do we find the child's book to be simply a *brief* of his father's? How often do we see in the former, nothing but an abstract of those principles which are detailed, illustrated and simplified in the latter? This is directly the reverse of what it should be. The child should not be thus dealt with. Because his little stomach cannot contain much, we should not take what is sufficient ſor a man and reduce it down to a concentrated essence, in order to bring it within the necessary compass. We should not only diminish the quantity, but should dilute the little which is given. We should go still more—much more into details and particulars. Instead of presenting to the child the roots of the whole bush, I would pluck a single living rose. We might then see his eyes sparkle with delight. But let it not be supposed, that any books can diminish the value of oral instruction. There is a power in the living voice which is to be ſound nowhere else. That most excellent use, the education of children, which is one of the great employments of the angels in heaven, is not likely to be held in too high estimation by men on earth. If it be desired to reach the child's understanding through his heart, the hearing is the direct way to effect it. Even when he reads his little volume himself, if it be read aright, his *internal hearing* will be alive and active, and he will seem to listen to a voice, though it may not be of this world. If the child be taught to *hear* in the true and full acceptation of that word, the great work is, as it were, accomplished. But who shall be trusted with that child's ear? In the spiritual world it is the office of the angels; and in this world it should be the office of those who are like the angels.

To illustrate the error to which I have alluded by an extreme case—viz. the error of making children's books too abstract—take the Assembly's Catechism. The same book which was designed for children, and is used by them, is the Creed and text book—*the abstract of the faith* of Orthodox churches. If there be any absurdity greater, it may perhaps be found in the contents of the work itself. A merciful Providence has thus permitted that falsities might possibly be innoxious. It is like poisonous fruit, which, if eaten whole, might perhaps pass off with little or no injury; whereas if it were first ground to powder, it would enter into the circulation, and derange or destroy the whole system. Although a bad way to teach truth, this is the best way in the world to teach falsities. If the false persuasions of the Old Church were permitted to be tasted and rel-

16*

ished by children, and thus become joined to their tender affections, the effect would indeed be dreadful. Hence this result has been providentially guarded against, by every possible means.

It is known to the New Church that eating and drinking correspond to that reception and appropriation of good and truth, in the will and understanding, in consequence of which they are brought forth into word and deed. This is not merely a pleasant analogy—it is rigorous truth; and we may therefore derive instruction as to the wants of the spiritual man and the manner in which they should be supplied, by attending to those of the body, and the way in which these are treated. We have already alluded to the necessity that exists, that the food should be reduced to its simple elements before it can enter into the system. After having undergone suitable preparation, first of all it is masticated. By this process it is ground as between two mill-stones, and being mixed with the saliva secreted for the purpose, by which its resolution is aided, in a pulpy state it is carried to the stomach. Here it is subjected to the operation of the gastric juice, and farther on to still other solvents, neither of which the art of chemistry is able to equal; till at last it is taken up and carried into the circulation by those very minute vessels, the lacteals. There is no room for *generalities* here. It has been a question among philosophers whether matter was infinitely divisible. Without considering this question in the abstract, I am almost ready to think it practically solved as the food is arrested and brought into direct subservience to the spirit.

But I wish to pursue this correspondence a little further; and will begin with the infant. We observe that he has no teeth. He is obliged to receive his food in a liquid form, and first of all from the breast of his mother. He not only does not *voluntarily* provide for himself, but can hardly be said to be *voluntary* in the appropriation of what is provided for him. He is nourished by his mother, with a substance on which her system has performed that labor which will not be required as his own is strengthened and matured.

And so precisely it is with the spirit. He is

overshadowed with his mother's love. How constantly is the child the object of her thoughts—and this not from effort, but from necessity. Here the memory is not treacherous. It needs no prompter. And the adaptation and correspondence between the wants of the child and the gifts of the mother, are not merely general, but though not observed they are minute and particular. The desire for food on the one part and the secretion of milk on the other, are simultaneous; and proceed from one and the same source. Does any one imagine that as the infant draws from the breast of his mother her milk, still warm with her own life, that his spirit is not also nourished and sustained by her affections? Does any one suppose that the Lord makes such wonderful provision for the body merely? If there are any such, I certainly shall not reason with them on the subject.

The almost immeasurable distance from the helplessness of infancy to the strength of manhood, must be passed by slow and imperceptible gradations. Although there may be distinct and remarkable eras, it is still one continuous path. After the child has left the breast of his mother, his appropriate food, though changed, is still similar. He still demands liquids, principally milk; and he is yet incapable of feeding himself. Gradually one tooth after another makes its appearance; and at length these give way to a firmer, stronger set, which from the very first were concealed beneath the others, patiently waiting their appointed time. And so it is with the spirit. His appropriate spiritual nourishment is that which has been elaborated in the minds of the attendant angels, and of his parents and instructers; and he receives it and ought to receive it, nothing doubting. He is not called upon to decide whether it is good and suitable for him. Of this it is the duty (and what a duty!) of others to judge. It is sufficient for him that it is provided by those whose place it is to provide. His duty is that of obedience—strict, willing obedience—and it should be the effort of his guardians on earth, as it is of his guardians in heaven, gradually and imperceptibly to disengage his hand from themselves, only that it may be given to Him whose right it is to lead. May we not hope that the desolation of a self-relying spirit which we have all of us experienced, may one day be spared to our children?

At an early age we observe indications of taste. The child desires food, and when it is given, it is received with a relish and satisfaction. This delight is the pledge of the use which the nourishment is intended to perform. If the child has not an appetite, we conclude at once that he is not well. We do not force him to eat the usual quantity, but take measures to remove the disease, that his disposition to receive nourishment may return.

And this leads me to the consideration of another error in the development of the mind, closely allied to the first on which I remarked. Those who are ready to cloy the young mind with generalities which it cannot comprehend, cannot of course be alive to the fact that spiritual food, not less than natural, in order to be useful should be tasted and relished. In the spiritual world children are instructed principally by representatives and correspondences. And what are the correspondences by which they are instructed? They are simply the affections of the attendant angels, embodied and presented in living forms of beauty. If the affection should cease but for an instant, the book would be closed and the lesson ended. And if love be the *substance* of that lesson, it must surely be learned with delight. Swedenborg's language on this subject is quite remarkable. He speaks "of infants in heaven being brought into the knowledges of truth and the affections of good, by representatives in use amongst them, as by sports suitable to their minds." He says that "all things are insinuated into them by delights and pleasantnesses which are suited to their temper." And in another place, "by pleasantnesses and delights they are introduced into the goods of innocence and charity, which goods are continually insinuated from the Lord by those delights and pleasantnesses." He also says, in the Arcana Cœlestia—

"Savory meats in the original language are the delights and pleasantnesses of taste, and signify, in the internal sense, the delights which are of good, and the pleasantnesses which are of truth, because the taste, as well as the other senses of the body, corresponds to celestial and spiritual things, of which correspondence, by the Divine Mercy of the Lord, we shall treat hereafter. It cannot be known how the case herein is, unless it be known in what manner the natural principle is made new, or receives life from the rational, i. e. from the Lord through the rational; the natural principle is not made new, or receives life corresponding with the rational, that is, is not regenerated, unless by doctrinals, or the knowledges of good and truth; the celestial man by the knowledges of good first, but the spiritual man by the knowledges of truth first; doctrinals, or the knowledges of good and truth, cannot be communicated to the natural man, thus cannot be conjoined and appropriated, unless by delights and pleasantnesses accommodated to it, for they are insinuated by an external or sensual way; whatsoever does not enter by some delight or pleasantness, does not inhere, thus does not continue."

If the instruction which is communicated is not received with delight, we may know that it is either unsuitable in itself, or that there is something wrong and disordered in the recipient. Our effort should be to ascertain where the difficulty is, and to remove it. It is of more importance that the child should have a truly healthy appetite, than that he should treasure up in his memory volumes by forced labor. But how totally this fact has been overlooked! To recur to the same book for illustration as in the former case, when did it ever enter into the imagination of man to conceive that the child could learn with pleasure and delight the contents of the Assembly's Catechism? Would not the real manifestation of these feelings be rebuked by the teachers of that book as unsuitable to the solemn nature of its contents? The angels who do continually look on the face of our Father in heaven, who are associated with children, and whose office it is to communicate good affections, and with them innocent delights, are here invited to withdraw, to make room for what is called religion.

But these remarks ought not perhaps to be made without a caution. There may be danger, in the New Church, lest the idea should gain ground that the child must have his own way—that he must always be left *in freedom*, and watched, but not governed. The freedom of the child is wrapped up in that of his parents and instructers; and that child cannot be *truly free* who does not feel their government, and give to it a full and willing obedience. Far be it from me to abate one jot or tittle of true order and discipline. They are above all price. But in order to be *true government*, it should influence the affections and not the fears. And if it be necessary that the love of the child should be tempered with fear, it should only be tempered, and not destroyed. That parent or instructer who rebukes a child or a pupil with feelings of personal unkindness or of anger, is guilty of a great sin. The evil should be seen and separated from the child, and the effort with us should be to remove it, as we should if it existed in our own minds. But those who are in the place of parents or instructers, who do not feel that the direction and government of their charge is *a duty*, are in danger of losing the power of discriminating between the good and the evil—the true and the false—not only in the minds of the children, but in their own. We should not attempt to cast out devils through Beelzebub the prince of devils; but it is not to be forgotten that they should be cast out in the name of the Lord.

Wordsworth expresses poetically a valuable truth, when he says that "the child is father of the man." In the infant mind are to be found the germ and rudiments of mature manhood. But it is not less true nor less obvious and important, that the man is father of the child. The mind is not to be developed by instinct merely, like animal life; nor by the heat and light of the natural sun, like a vegetable. It demands the experience and knowledges of other minds. It requires to be warmed by the affections and enlightened by the understandings of those whose duty it is to watch over it. The idea which has to some extent obtained, that the child should be left free to the formation of his religious sentiments—that the affections need only to be stimulated to a development of themselves, and not aided and directed, is absurd and cruel.

The absurdity of this practice would be sufficiently obvious if carried into the study of any one of the natural sciences. How would it do to take the child into the labaratory of the chemist, and leave him to make his own combinations, try his own experiments and draw his own results, unbiassed by the opinions of others? Some sad accident would soon bear testimony to the rashness of such a course. And does he need no guidance and direction on spiritual subjects? Or is it because the spirit and not the body is wounded, that any are blind to the injury that is sustained?

Such is not the true course. The child needs instruction on spiritual subjects. He is in a state to receive truth when presented, but this presentation cannot well be dispensed with. His first lesson should be that of humility, and a willingness to be led and instructed by others—or rather this disposition should be cherished as the ground of every lesson. Any who would rob him of this, are enemies to his spiritual life. Instead of teaching him that he needs no aid from others, he should become sensible that he is weak and feeble, and must receive every thing from others. Instead of telling him that all that is wanted is the exercise of his own reason and understanding, his opinion should never be asked, nor the truths he is taught ever permitted to be called in question. If his instructer is sensible of giving him pure water to drink, he will not willingly allow the suspicion that it is unclean. Instead of stimulating the child to throw off his nature in the vain attempt to ape the man, the instructer should himself become a child and meet his pupil on his own ground, imparting wisdom without doing violence to his simplicity.

It is not because spiritual truths are so plain and simple, and so well understood in the world, that the idea exists that the child should be left to himself. Far otherwise. It is because all is doubt and darkness and confusion, on spiritual subjects in mature minds, that the foolish fantasy has arisen, that all is day-light in the mind of the child. Does any one suppose, that if spiritual truths were as settled and incontrovertible as scientific, that it would ever have entered the imaginations of any to pursue such a course? If the instructer have truth to give, why does he withhold it on the most important of all subjects? If he have light, why does he put it under a bushel? Such is not the order of heaven nor of a true church—when falsities and not truths exist, it may be permitted for good.

I trust that the fact that truths should be implanted in the affections and received with delight, will in no one encourage the thought that the mind of the child is naturally pure and only needs to be developed, without being regenerated. We learn from the doctrines of the New Church, that the mind is naturally filled with hereditary evils; but these are at first quiescent, and are permitted to appear only by degrees, as there is ability to see and power to resist them. The child is under the influence of the angels, and is suffered to partake of their innocence and happiness. Afterwards, evil affections make their appearance, and these also have their delights; and there would be no ability to resist them, unless the delights of good had been miraculously imparted, before. If the parents and instructers discriminate between the good and the evil in the child, he may at an early age be made to co-operate in the same work in himself—we hardly know how early. The good affections, which are constantly imparted by the Lord, are to be brought forth into corresponding works and objects—the evil, which are from the opposite source, are to be resisted and put away.

It is obvious that with the New Church a totally new field is opened for the instruction of children—unexplored and bounded only by the heavens. But though unexplored, it is not pathless. We are not required to make the way; but only to be willing to travel in the right direction. Time and eternity are again joined together, not merely in name, but in fact. The child is not to be taught his catechism, in the promise and expectation of a distant reward in the future state. He is not to put on the sad formalities of religion, in the vain hope that his weeds may hereafter be turned into joy The heavens are now uncovered. It is permitted to those who think it an object worthy of their attention, to look into them—to learn the laws and affections by which they are governed; and from a distinct revelation of the end to be attained, to understand the means by which it is to be effected. The question is brought home—

what is really of use to the child—what hereditary or actual evils are to be removed—what good to be imparted—what truth to be communicated. He has commenced a journey, where the end and the way are now distinctly revealed; and the veil of death which has hitherto limited his vision, should hereafter only temper and accommodate the brightness and glory which are beyond.